And it came to pass in those days, that there went out a
decree from Caesar Augustus, that all the world should be
taxed. And all went to be taxed, every one into his own
city. And this taxing was first made when Cyrenius was
Governer of Syrie. And Joseph also went up from Galilee,
out of the city of Nazareth, into Judea, unto the city of
David, which is called Bethlehem; (because he was of the
house and lineage of David:) To be taxed with Mary his
espoused wife, being great with child. And so it was, that,
while they were there, the days were accomplished that she
should be delivered. And she brought forth her firstborn
son, and wrapped him in swaddling clothes, and laid him in
a manger; because there was no room for them in the inn.
And there were in the same country shepherds abiding in
the field, keeping watch over their flock by night. And, lo,
the angel of the Lord came upon them, and the glory of the
Lord shone round about them: and they were sore afraid.
And the angel said unto them, Fear not: for, behold, I bring
you good tidings of great joy, which shall be to all people.

For unto you is born this day in the city of David a Saviour, which is Christ the Lord. And this shall be a sign unto you; Ye shall find the babe wrapped in swaddling clothes, lying in a manger. And suddenly there was with the angel a multitude of the heavenly host praising God, and saying, Glory to God in the highest, and on earth peace to men of goodwill. And it came to pass, as the angels were gone away from them into heaven, the shepherds said one to another, Let us go even unto Bethlehem, and see this thing which is come to pass, which the Lord hath made known unto us. And they came with haste, and found Mary, and Joseph, and the baby lying in a manger. And when they had seen it, they made known abroad the saying which was told them concerning this child. And all they that heard it wondered at those things which were told them by the shepherds. But Mary kept all these things, and pondered them in her heart.

Luke 2: 1-20

THE SUGAR-PLUM CHRISTMAS BOOK

THE SUGAR-PLUM CHRISTMAS BOOK

A BOOK FOR CHRISTMAS AND ALL THE DAYS OF THE YEAR

JEAN CHAPMAN

Illustrated by

DEBORAH NILAND

Song Settings by

Margaret Moore

CHILDRENS PRESS INTERNATIONAL
CHICAGO

1983 School and Library Edition
First published in 1977
by Hodder and Stoughton (Australia) Pty Ltd
2 Apollo Place, Lane Cove, NSW 2066
Reprinted 1978
Reprinted 1981
© text Jean Chapman 1977 *children's Press*
© illustrations Deborah Niland 1977
© musical settings Hodder and Stoughton (Australia) Pty Ltd 1977

National Library of Australia Cataloguing-in-Publication entry

Chapman, Jean, comp.

The sugar-plum christmas book.
Index.
For children.
1. Christmas — Juvenile literature. I. Chapman, Jean, comp. II. Niland, Deborah, illus. III. Moore, Margaret. *I, Title*

J 394.268282

Printed in Hong Kong

INTRODUCTION

CHRISTMAS as we know it today is a many-faceted festival. On one hand, a joyous holy day, a spiritual celebration of Christ's nativity; on another, a feast of pagan origins dedicated, in modern terms, to commercial profit; and, again, it is a time of reunion for family and friends, of general goodwill, of indulgence, of sugar plums and secular holiday. All these facets are intermingled: while children and grown-ups sing carols in church on Christmas morning, their thoughts, at the same time, may perhaps just stray for one moment or two towards the giving and receiving of gifts, the Christmas dinner cooking in the oven, the bonus added to the pre-Christmas pay-packet, the fortnight's holiday planned for the new year. . . . Sometimes this admixture is deplored, and one hears a lament that 'the true spirit of Christmas is no longer with us'. And yet — it would seem that this intermingling of the spiritual and the secular has existed right from the beginning, when Jesus Himself was born, during a journey undertaken in the interests of the Roman census and tax-collector. This prosaic background to the Nativity, however, in no way dims the glory of Jesus' birth, the adoration of the shepherds, the homage of the three kings.

At the dawn of the Christian era, the choice of 25th December as Christmas Day conveniently submerged within the Church calendar such ancient pagan feasts as the celebration of the Winter Solstice and the Roman Lupercalia. It was, of course, a choice made in the colder region of the northern hemisphere: in spite of geographical fact, we have ever since sung carols which describe the mild winter of Bethlehem in terms of the frozen north, while Australians, adhering to the geographical myth in another fashion, resolutely eat piping-hot Christmas dinners in sweltering summer weather. (Joan Mellings' poem, on page 59, nicely presents the differing temperature of Christmas in two hemispheres.)

This collection, made with young children in mind, includes stories, both traditional and original, carols, poems and practical activities which together present a wide-angled view of Christmas. Based firmly upon the Nativity as related in the New Testament, the contents range over all those delightful customs and enjoyments we associate with Christmas: carol singing, trimming the Christmas tree, present-giving with its secrets and crackling of paper, feasting and pantomime. And (as, for instance, in the Russian tale of Baboushka, the Dutch story of St Nicholas, the German tradition of Julklapp), this collection presents, as well, glimpses of Christmas in many far-flung places, including European traditions and customs which have helped to enrich the Australian celebration of Christmas, brought here by settlers from other lands.

An older Bible version of the Nativity story, which can be used with very young children, has been included in the collection, rather than a new translation. The Nativity story readily divides in three parts: the collection begins with Jesus' birth, an event within the understanding of the youngest child; it goes on to tell the story of the shepherds, and then the coming of the Magi.

Any Christmas anthology is bound to leave out some favourite sugar plum — why not add your own favourite carols, stories and traditions to this book? You may like to retell in your own words some of the stories already in the collection, too. As in Jean Chapman's two previous collections for young children, TELL ME A TALE and TELL ME ANOTHER TALE, she shows a very special empathy, expert knowledge, and sheer enjoyment of the world of young children — and has given them another book to delight in, not only at Christmas time, but all the year round. The overall spirit of this book is, perhaps, best summed up by these words from Zoe McHenry's Australian carol, *Christmas Bells*:

Christmas is giving time, Christmas is loving time.

Barbara Ker Wilson

For You
and for Dinks,
who loved
children and Christmas

Acknowledgements
The extract *Sing Joy*, from *Our Brother Is Born*, from *The Oxford Book of Carols*, is reproduced by permission of the Oxford University Press.
The poem *Christmas in Two Lands* is reprinted by kind permission of the author and Paul Hamlyn (Australia) Pty Ltd.

CONTENTS

Key to Symbols for contents

☼ = story   ✩ = verse

🔔 = activity   🎵 = song

✩	A Good Time Is Coming	11
✩	Music While You Sing	11
✩	Sing Joy *Eleanor Farjeon*	13
🎵	Blow The Trumpet *Traditional carol, France*	14
☼	The First Christmas	16
🔔	A Crèche To Make	20
🔔	Flour Paste	23
✩	Birthday Gift *Christina Rossetti*	23
☼	The Shepherds	24
✩	Long Long Ago *Traditional carol, England*	26
🔔	Shepherds To Make	26
☼	Guiding Star	27
🔔	Three Kings To Make	30
🔔	Bright Star, Light Star, Make A Star	31
🔔	Gathering Stars	33
✩	On A Blue Hill *Traditional rhyme, England*	34
☼	A Lamb Of Bethlehem *A story from Syria*	35
🔔	A Lamb To Make	38
✩	Old Donkey And Ox And Little Grey Sheep	39
🔔	Eat Well! Sleep Well!	40
🔔	Nisse Finger-puppet	41
🔔	In-a-minute Puppets	42

🎄 STICKY-STICK PUPPETS — 44
🎄 RINGS ON EACH FINGER — 44
☆ SHALL I TELL YOU? — 45
❄ ROBIN'S RED BREAST — 46
✡ BREAD AND MILK   *Christina Rossetti* — 48
🎄 REMEMBER THE BIRDS — 49
🎄 BIRD TREE — 50
❄ SILVERY SPIDERY TREE   *A Story from Germany* — 51
🎄 TREES TO MAKE — 54
☆ RITSCH, RATSCH FILIBOM!   *Traditional carol, Sweden* — 58
☆ CHRISTMAS IN TWO LANDS   *Joan Mellings* — 59
❄ THE LITTLE JUGGLER OF CHARTRES — 60
🎄 THIS IS THE CHURCH — 65
🎄 CATCH THE BELL RINGER — 66
❄ WHO REMEMBERED JOANNA? — 67
🎄 BELLS TO MAKE — 70
☆ WELCOME   *Traditional song, Czechoslovakia* — 73
❄ THE WAY OF WISHES — 74
☆ IF WISHES WERE HORSES   *Traditional rhyme, England* — 81
🎄 LUCKY WISHBONES — 81
🎄 WISHING HARP — 82
☆ STAR-LIGHT, STAR-BRIGHT — 82
☆ WASH THE DISHES   *Traditional rhyme, England* — 83
☆ PARCEL — 83
❄ JULKLAPP! — 84
🎄 PLAY DOUGH — 89
🎄 DECORATIONS TO MAKE — 89
☆ THE GINGERBREAD MAN   *Traditional street cry, England* — 90
🎄 WALNUTS AND MATCHES — 90

♧ THE PARTY   91

🍄 JOLLY SMILING COOK   94

🍄 GOODIES TO MAKE   95

✡ DECISION   98

♧ SKY HIGH PIE   *A story from England*   99

✡ ST THOMAS' DAY IS PAST AND GONE   *Traditional song, England* 101

✡ LITTLE JACK HORNER   102

🍄 JACK HORNER'S PLUM   102

🍄 THE PLUM GAME   102

🍄 BONBONS TO MAKE   103

🍄 GAMES TO PLAY   104

✡ SING, SING   *Traditional rhyme, England*   106

✡ CHRISTMAS PUDDING   *Traditional song, England*   107

♧ LITTLE PLUM DUFF   108

✡ FRUITY PERCY   112

🍄 A PUDDING TO MAKE   112

♧ THE RED CAP   113

🐝 NASTY LITTLE BEASTIES   119

✡ SNOWFLAKES FALLING   120

🍄 SNOWFLAKES TO MAKE   120

🍄 PAPER AND CARDS TO MAKE   121

🍄 A RING OF ANGELS TO MAKE   126

♧ THE SECRET   127

🐝 I WISH YOU A MERRY CHRISTMAS   *Traditional song, England*   130

🍄 SOME PRESENTS TO MAKE   131

♧ PINK SUGAR MOUSE   133

✡ SUGAR AND SPICE AND LITTLE PINK MICE   *Traditional rhyme, England*   137

🍄 THUMB MOUSE   138

A Toe Filled With Gold   *A story from Turkey* — 139

Find Us Quickly If You Can   *Traditional rhyme, Holland* — 141

A Nicholas Sack — 141

A Super Stocking — 142

Memory Game — 143

A Visit From St Nicholas   *Clement Moore* — 144

Sing! Dance!   *Traditional carol, Spain* — 146

Steffan Was A Stable Boy   *Traditional rhyme, Sweden* — 147

Christmas   *Peter Cornelius* — 148

The Day After Christmas — 149

The Nutcracker — 153

Christmas Boxes — 157

Piggy Bank — 157

Could It Be? — 159

Slip, Slide, Swooooosh! — 160

New Year   *Traditional rhyme, England* — 163

Shortbread — 165

Hogmanay Cake   *A story from Scotland* — 166

Tick-Tock — 173

All In The Morning   *Traditional song, England* — 173

Twelfth Night Song   *Traditional song, Russia* — 174

Twelfth Night — 175

Sing A Song Of Sixpence — 176

Baboushka — 177

Baboushka Doll — 182

A Partridge In A Pear Tree — 184

Come Again   *Traditional song, France* — 187

A Round Of Bells — 188

Index — 189

A GOOD TIME IS COMING

A good time is coming, I wish it were here!
The very best time for the whole of the year!
I'm counting each day on my fingers and thumbs
The days that will pass before Christmas time comes.

I'll hang up my stocking, in case Santa brings
A rosy red apple and other good things.
And he knows how dearly I love sugar plums —
I'd like a big box full when Christmas time comes.

Elizabeth Fill

MUSIC WHILE YOU SING

What sweeter music can we bring
Than a carol, for to sing.

Robert Herrick

A carol is a song of joy. Many carols are sung all the year round, but those most loved belong to Christmas time. Some are very old; in days gone by, people used to dance to their toe-tapping tunes. Nowadays, carols are sung in churches, in shops and houses, by carol-singers in the streets, on the radio and television, and, in some parts of Australia, outdoors — when people gather in parks or gardens during the hot summer nights of Christmas time, with lighted candles, to sing together.

Here are some ways to make music while you sing:

Trumpet   Fold a circle of paper into a cone shape. Cut off the pointed end to make a small hole. Now blow.
Ta-d'da! Ta-d'da! Ta-d'da-da-daaah!

Drum   A tin or a plastic container can be turned upside-down and beaten with fingers, clenched fists, a pencil, a spoon or anything which makes a good sound.
Boom-boom! Boom-a-boom! Boom!

Blocks   Bang small blocks of wood against each other, or try clonking together the open ends of two paper cups.
Klop-klop-klop-kerlop!

Maracas   Click walnuts together. For another kind of sound clink two metal spoons. Wooden spoons make a softer, lower-toned kind of music.
Click-click-clonk-click!

Bells   Be careful with this one, otherwise there may be cracked or broken glass and cut fingers, but you can gently tap a metal spoon against a glass or a bottle for a tinkling sound.
Ring-a-ting-ting!

Sticks   Tap one stick against another stick. Pencils and rulers work well, too.

12

	Tap! Tap! Tap-tap-tap-tap-tap!
Cymbals	Two saucepan lids can be clashing cymbals. *Classssssssssh!*
Woofer	Try blowing across the opening in the top of a long-necked bottle. It's spooky. *Warr! Warrr!*
Kazoo	This will tickle your lips. Wrap a scrap of tissue-paper about a clean comb. Blow a tune through the paper. The sound will be as funny as the name *cazoo*. *Zzzzz! Zz-z-zz! Z-z-z-z-zzzzz! Zzzzzz!*

And if you want to, you can slap your thighs, clap your hands, click your tongue, pop a cheek with a finger and stamp your feet. You are sure to think of other ways to make different sounds. Can you whistle? Can you hum? What else can you do?

SING JOY

Sing sweet as a flute,
Sing clear as a horn,
Sing joy of the children
Come Christmas Morn.

Eleanor Farjeon

Here is a French carol to sing. At the same time play the instruments you've made, or pretend to blow a trumpet or beat a drum.

BLOW THE TRUMPET

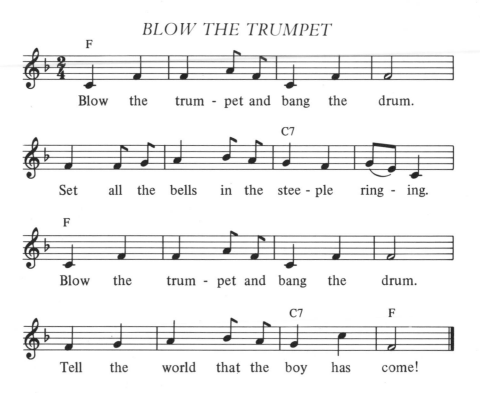

Blow the trum - pet and bang the drum.

Set all the bells in the stee - ple ring - ing.

Blow the trum - pet and bang the drum.

Tell the world that the boy has come!

Blow the whistle
And bang the blocks,
Set all the tambourines in hands tinkling.
Blow the whistle
And bang the blocks,
Tell the world
That the boy has come!

Shake maracas
And click the sticks,
Set all the golden cymbals a-jingling.
Shake maracas,
And click the sticks,
Tell the world
That the boy has come!

Blow the trumpet
And bang the drum,
Set all the bells
In the steeple ringing.
Blow the trumpet
And bang the drum,
Tell the world
That the boy has come.

Who is the boy in the carol?
He was the baby named Jesus.
The first of all Christmas days was his birthday, hundreds of
years ago. The story of the first Christmas has been told ever
since. And this is how some little children first hear it.

THE FIRST CHRISTMAS

Long ago, a man called Joseph, who was a carpenter, left his house to journey to the town of Bethlehem, to pay his taxes. Mary, his wife, wanted to go with him although she was soon to have a baby. So Joseph found a donkey for Mary to ride.

Clip-*clop!* Clippity-*clop!* They travelled on and on, over rough roads until the end of the day. Clip . . . clop . . . *clop!*

Mary watched the sun slip down behind the hills. Already it was cold. And it would become colder as the night came. Off the road in the fields, shepherds had lit small fires and huddled about them, warming their hands and feet. Near the shepherds the sheep were crowding together, settling for the night.

Mary longed to stop, but on they must go to Bethlehem.

Clop . . . *clop!* Clop . . . *c-c-clop!* The donkey was walking slower and slower. His head drooped. He was too tired to lift it. Mary was heavy on his back, so heavy now.

Joseph looked at his wife. He saw her tiredness and he wished their journey was over, so that Mary could rest before the baby was born. He peered ahead but there was no sign of the town. No twinkling lamps. No fires glowing in the night. Only darkness.

16

Reaching up, Joseph patted the donkey's shoulder, saying, "It can't be much farther, old friend! Not much farther!"

And not long afterwards they did see Bethlehem.

Soon they were clattering over the town's narrow streets. *Clip*-clop-*clippity*-clop! They went to an inn where travellers stayed. Its door was shut.

Joseph knocked, and he knocked again and again before the sleepy inn-keeper dragged open the door. In the light of his lantern the man blinked and squinted up at Mary, who pulled her old dust-soiled cloak about her. The inn-keeper then glanced at Joseph, whose back was bent with weariness; he hardly noted the donkey at all as he yawned, "You can't stay here. The place is full up."

"But I must find somewhere my wife can rest," said Joseph. "Her baby will be born soon. Please, can't you help?"

"No!" the inn-keeper yawned again and scratched his chest. "I told you there's no room. The inn is full. Too many people are staying in Bethlehem tonight." And he stepped backwards as if to close the door. Instead, however, he waited a moment and now he gave the donkey a long look, and said: "You can put the donkey in the stable. And you can stay there too, if you like. It's not much but it's empty. That's all I can offer."

"A stable isn't—" began Joseph, but the inn-keeper was gone with a loud slam of the door, and Mary was calling after him, "Thank you, thank you!" Perhaps he heard her through the closed door.

Then she turned to Joseph. "We'll go to the stable. It will be warm there," she said. "There's sure to be clean straw we can sleep on."

So they went to the stable, the shelter-shed for the animals belonging to the inn.

While Joseph made Mary a bed from straw, a cow came to watch him strew it on the ground. The cow still watched as Joseph covered Mary with his cloak; she could hear the cow munching contentedly at her cud. And Mary heard other small sounds too: the feet of cattle brushing the straw, the swish of a tail, the donkey drinking the water Joseph had given him.

No sounds drifted into the stable from the inn or the town, and soon Mary and Joseph slept.

Late in the night Mary woke, and her baby was born. She wrapped Him in the soft clothes which she had brought with her to Bethlehem. And Joseph made the Baby a cradle-bed in one of the old wooden feeding-boxes belonging to the cattle. He filled the manger with clean sweet straw.

As Mary put the Baby into the manger-bed, Joseph smiled at her. "His name will be Jesus," he said. And as he spoke, Mary saw over his shoulder a patch of night sky above the stable door. It was bright with stars, stars and more stars; glinting twinkling stars, bright sparkling stars. And far away, from amongst the stars, voices seemed to be singing. Or was it only the wind in the trees?

Mary sang her own song then. It was a little crooning song, a lullaby for Baby Jesus. It was a song of gladness for the first of all Christmas days.

HELLO

A CRÊCHE TO MAKE

The birthday of Jesus is remembered in many different ways. A special scene showing the stable on the first Christmas morning is often set up in a church or a special place. It may be in a park, or a shop window, or a town square. Many people like to make their own stable scene. Often it is called a *crêche*. A crêche always includes figures of Mary and Joseph as well as Baby Jesus. The figures may be the size of real people and animals—often the stable animals are included, too. Sometimes the figures are very small, made from clay or wood, plastic or metal. You can make a crêche for yourself from scrap materials. Or you could make a crêche for someone's Christmas present. Here are some ideas.

The stable A box, perhaps a shoe-box, turned on one side can be the stable. Does it need a roof? A piece of corrugated cardboard put over the top makes a flat roof. Cardboard can be bent across the middle to make a peaked shape if you like that better.
Fasten the roof with some sticky tape.
Paint the stable if you want to, and put some shredded paper or straw on the floor.
Decorate the outside with some bare twigs and small sprays of tiny leaves. Sticky tape or glue will keep them firm.

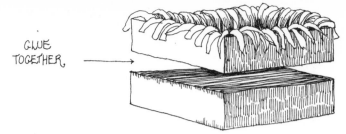

GLUE TOGETHER

The manger   The stable needs a manger-bed. The trays of two match-boxes glued together by the bottoms can be the manger. Fill it with shredded paper, cotton wool or wisps of straw. Now find the best place to stand it in the stable.

The Babe   The manger needs a baby. If you haven't a tiny doll make one from a piece of match-stick, or a twig. Wrap it in a strip of paper tissue, or cloth. Another idea is to use a jelly baby sweet. Now the babe can sleep in the manger-bed.

Mary and Joseph   You can dress dolls or make figures from cardboard cones, or plastic bottles. Clothes-peg dolls are quickly made. You need wooden dolly pegs for Mary and Joseph. Twist a pipe-cleaner about each clothes-peg to make arms. On the round top of the pegs draw faces with a felt pen, paint or crayons.

Mary's dress is a scrap of blue material, or a blue paper tissue folded into half. Cut the tissue to make it as long as the peg and twice as wide. Now you can make a little slit in the fold and fit the dress over Mary's head. Tie a ribbon about her waist and pull her arms free. Another scrap of material or tissue makes a cloak. Fold it over her head.

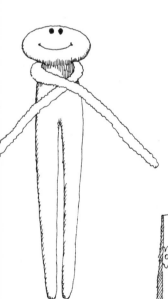
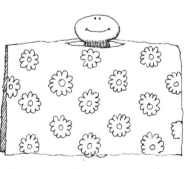

Mary is ready to stand in the crêche, close to the manger.

Joseph can be dressed in the same way as Mary, but use a different material. He doesn't need a cloak. You can give him wool-fluff hair, or make it from shredded paper or cotton wool. Colour it with paint. Does Joseph need a beard? You decide, then stand him in the stable too. The dolls' feet may need to be pushed into a blob of clay or plasticine to keep them upright.

The star

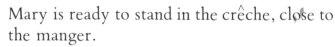

Decorate the stable roof with a star. Twist three or four pipe-cleaners into a star shape. You may have some coloured ones.

To make the star glisten, twine some strands of tinsel over its points, or use thin streamers of cooking foil. Now the star is ready to shine from the stable roof. Fasten it firmly with sticky tape or ask someone to help you to secure it with a drawing-pin.

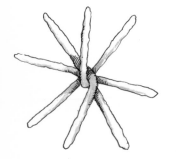

FLOUR PASTE

1 cup of plain flour
½ teaspoon of salt
Cold water

Slowly mix the flour and salt with enough water to thicken it.
Heat the mixture slowly, stirring all the time, until the paste leaves the sides of the pot.
Add a little more water if it is too thick.
Cool, then use.
Keep your paste in an airtight container.

BIRTHDAY GIFT

What can I give Him
    Poor as I am?
If I were a shepherd
I would bring Him a lamb.
If I were a Wise Man
I would do my part.
Yet what can I give Him?
    Give my heart.

          Christina Rossetti

THE SHEPHERDS

The night that Jesus was born, some shepherds were in the hill fields of Bethlehem. Perhaps in the twilight they had seen Mary and Joseph pass along the road. Who knows now? It was long ago. And at that time many people were travelling to Bethlehem. The little town was crowded.

It was winter time and it was cold. The sheep moved together to keep warm. The shepherds pulled their thick cloaks tightly about them when they came to sit by their fire. One shepherd walked about, watching the sheep. He stamped his feet and rubbed his chilled hands, and he listened to a young shepherd lad playing softly on a pipe.

One of the oldest shepherds also listened to the boy's tune. Then he drowsed. His head fell on his chest. Soon he was snoring. The others let him sleep while they talked in low voices about their work and the news of the day.

Suddenly a great light filled the sky. The field was as bright as morning. The shepherds were startled. They shielded their eyes with their arms and staggered to their feet, pulling the snoring shepherd with them. He called out in alarm and the young shepherd dropped his pipe as they all pulled back, afraid of what they now saw.

It was an angel.

"Fear not!" the angel told them. "I bring joy to you and all people. Unto you this night is born a child."

A child? The shepherds were too astonished to speak. Their mouths could not find words. Their lips moved but no sounds came.

As if the angel knew their thoughts he said, "In the City of David is a saviour, who is Christ the Lord."

The City of David was another name for Bethlehem. It was close by, just across the fields. It was here, in the stable of an inn, that the shepherds would find the child.

The angel finished speaking and the splendid light about him grew stronger, brighter and more beautiful. The air filled with the music of singing voices: "Glory to God in the highest, and on earth peace and goodwill towards men!"

The music rang out over the fields and the hills and the sky. Then, little by little, it faded . . . faded away. And the great light dimmed until the shepherds were alone in the field once more. A sheep bleated and darkness was about them.

Perhaps they took a lamb with them as a present for the baby in the stable. Many people say they did, as they went hurrying off to find the child.

And when Mary showed them the sleeping baby they told her of the angel, the singing voices and the splendid light which had lit their field. Then with glad hearts they went back to their sheep, and Mary sat quietly thinking over all they had told her.

LONG, LONG AGO

Wind through the olive trees softly did blow
Round little Bethlehem long long ago.
Sheep on the hillside lay white in the snow
Shepherds were watching them, long long ago.
Shepherds were watching them, long long ago.

Then from the happy skies, angels bent low,
Singing their songs of joy, long long ago.
There, in His manger-bed, cradled, we know,
Christ came to Bethlehem, long long ago.
Christ came to Bethlehem, long long ago.

SHEPHERDS TO MAKE

Put some shepherds in the crêche you have made. Make as many as you like, dressing them like Joseph. Some can wear cloaks. Some can have beards. Some can wear short headdresses made from a square of material fastened with a band of cotton or string.

Let each shepherd carry a crook, a stick with a hooked end which the shepherd used with his sheep. Your shepherds could carry crooks made from pipe-cleaners. Bend one end of each cleaner to make a hook, and the crook is ready to hang over a shepherd's arm. You may need to bend his pipe-cleaner arm a little to hold it. If the crook is too long, trim it to size.

GUIDING STAR

Hundreds of years ago, there lived three wise men.

One was Melchior. He was small and old. His beard was long and grey.

Then there was Caspar. He was the youngest of the three. Caspar was tall. His back was straight and broad. Caspar had no beard.

The third wise man was Balthazar; he was neither old nor young. Balthazar had dark skin. His eyes were dark, his hair was dark. Balthazar walked in long, strong strides.

These three wise men had known for a long time that a great king was to be born. He would be the King of Kings, greater than any other the world had known. Men would not forget his kindness and wisdom and his love for people. Yet, great as this king would be, the wise men did not know when or where he would be born. So they waited for a sign.

At last the sign came. It was a brilliant star which shone as

27

if ablaze; sharp eyes could find it even in the daylight sky. And it shone from a part of the sky where no other star had shone before.

"We have seen His star," said the wise men. "The King is born!" And they set out to find Him, not knowing where He was, but carrying precious gifts for the new baby prince.

They rode on camels. Resting by day, they travelled by night, following the star as it crossed the dark sky. They followed the star through many lands, and at last it brought them to the city of Jerusalem. As the wise men rode through the city's streets the star was fading in the light of morning; the travellers thought their journey had ended.

People hurried from houses to stare at the camels which swayed by, their riders perched high on the beasts' humped backs. They stared at the strangeness of the travellers' rich clothing, but stranger still were the questions the wise men asked. "Where is He who is born to be king?" they wanted to know. "We have seen His star in the east, and we have travelled far to find Him."

The people shook their heads. There was no royal baby in Jerusalem. Only King Herod was at the palace. No prince had been born.

Soon Herod himself heard of the three wise men who sought a royal child. He was troubled. Would a new king take over his kingdom? What then would happen to him? He was afraid. Cunningly he bade the travellers come before him and tell all they knew of the prince they were seeking. "Search diligently," he ordered them then, "and when you find the Child, bring me word, that I may come and see Him."

So the three wise men left Jerusalem. Again they found the star. It shone above their heads in the night sky.

It moved on, leading them to Bethlehem, until it stood over the stable where the Child was. A stable! A stable behind an inn. The wise men had expected a palace.

But grey old Melchior knelt down in the straw beside the manger-bed. And Caspar and Balthazar knelt with him. They opened their saddle-bags to give Mary the precious gifts they had carried so far for the little boy. There was gold in one casket. Another held frankincense, a rare and beautiful perfume. And a golden horn was filled with myrrh, another precious scent.

The long journey of the wise men had ended.

Melchior, Caspar and Balthazar did not go back to King Herod to tell him that the Christ Child could be found in a Bethlehem stable. They did not trust Herod. Instead, they took a different road to return to their own lands. And the guiding star which had led them to Bethlehem disappeared from the sky.

THREE KINGS TO MAKE

Is there room in your crêche for the Three Wise Men? They can be made from pegs and pipe-cleaners, too. Very often they are dressed like kings, so find richly coloured materials or papers to make their long cloaks. Perhaps you'll be able to find some braids, bright string, sequins or scraps of fur to trim their clothes.

Remember that it was Melchior who had a long grey beard. Use a scrap of cotton wool to make that.

Balthazar had dark hair and dark skin. You may want to paint his face brown. Often he is shown wearing a magnificent turban. A length of gold embroidery thread with two different-coloured pipe-cleaners can be twisted about Balthazar's head into a turban shape. Purple and red look rich with the gold, but you may like other colours better. Make the turban sparkle by pinning to it a beautiful button or bead.

Melchior and Caspar can wear royal crowns made from silver or gold paper or cardboard dusted with glitter and sequins.

Perhaps you can find something each wise man can carry as his gift. Again, a button may be right. Or a tiny Christmas tree decoration. Look about and see what you can find.

One last thing . . . the wise men can stand on different-sized balls of clay or plasticine so they are not all the same height.

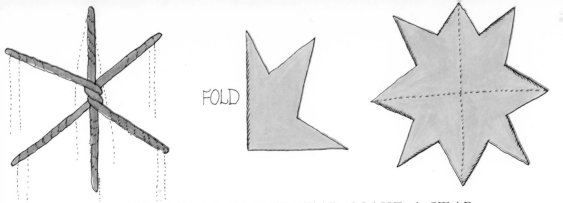

FOLD

BRIGHT STAR, LIGHT STAR, MAKE A STAR

Often a star shines from the top of a Christmas tree. It is a reminder of the great star which guided the Three Wise Men to Bethlehem.

Spiky star   One way to make a Christmas star is to twist some pipe-cleaners together by their middles, then spread out the ends into a star shape. Twine tinsel or very fine strips of foil about the star, then hang it in a doorway or a window, or give it away as a present.

Silver star   A star can be cut from kitchen foil or a foil pie-plate.
Fold the foil into four.
Cut the star's points.
Unfold the foil, and there's the star.

Glitter star   A glittering, glistening star begins as five triangles of thin cardboard. Be sure to cut the triangles the same size. The first one cut can be the pattern for the rest.
Glue the triangles into a star shape by overlapping the pointed ends.
Brush glue over the star, then sprinkle it with glitter.
Now hang it on a tree.

31

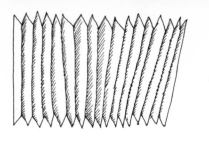
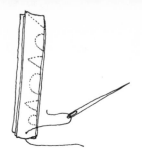

Snowflake star	This star is harder to make. A grown-up will help you with it, if need be, but try to make it by yourself. See how you get on.

Snowflake star

This star is harder to make. A grown-up will help you with it, if need be, but try to make it by yourself. See how you get on.
Cut a long strip of paper. It should be four times longer than it is wide.
Pleat the paper like a fan.
On *one* side only snip out small pieces to make a snowflake pattern.
Now cut across the top end to make it slanted.
Thread cotton through the bottom.
Unfold the paper.
Pull the cotton firmly and let the paper spread out into a star shape. The long cotton end is now in the centre of the star. Fasten it off with a couple of knots and the star is ready to hang up.

Straw star

Take six or eight drinking-straws and build them into a star shape. Staple or sew the centre to keep the straws in place. Dip the ends into glue and then into glitter to make the star twinkle. This star looks smart and jaunty if striped straws are cut in uneven lengths.

There are sure to be other ways you can find to make Christmas stars.

GATHERING STARS:
A game to play with friends

Any number of children can play. First, decide who the Star Gatherer will be. The rest of the players are the stars.

The stars line up some way off from the Star Gatherer. They will run across a pretend sky, past the Gatherer to a place *behind* him.

However, not one star must move, not a foot or a leg until the Gatherer asks,

"Stars, Stars, Stars so bright!
How many stars shine tonight?"

The Stars answer,

"More Stars than you can catch!
More Stars than you can snatch!"

Away run the stars! Helter-skelter!

But watch out, Stars! The star Gatherer is off too, running after them. If a Star is caught then that Star becomes a Star Gatherer as well.

And so the game goes on and on until there's not a star left to cross the sky.

What happens then?

The game begins all over again.

33

ON A BLUE HILL

White sheep, white sheep,
On a blue hill,
When the wind stops
You stand so still.
When the wind blows
You walk away slow.
White sheep, white sheep,
Where do you go?

A LAMB OF BETHLEHEM

After the shepherds had visited the Christ Child, soon after He was born, on their way back to their sheep they told every one they met of the marvels of that night.

Soon, more and more people were crowding about them, wanting to hear about the baby born in the stable. And all the time, while the shepherds talked, their sheep cropped the grass about them.

Two lambs had moved close to the shepherds and they heard the story each time it was told. After a while the bigger lamb said, "I would like to see the Christ Child for myself."

"Nothing is found unless it is looked for," said the smaller lamb. "We look for the grass we eat. We look for the water we drink. So we can look for the Christ Child. We could go tonight."

I'M GOING TO SEE WHAT IS ON THE NEXT PAGE

At dusk, before it was too dark, they slipped away from the other sheep, springing and skipping down the hill. Before long they came to a shepherds' hut. "Is the Child in there?" asked the bigger lamb. "Is this the stable where the shepherds saw Him?"

"Nothing is found unless it is looked for," said the little lamb. *Bump!* He butted his head against the closed door. It creaked open, just enough for the little lamb to poke his head into the hut. It was empty. "The Child isn't here," he said. "Come on! We'll look somewhere else."

They went to the road.

Platter-plat-platter-plat! Their feet sounded strange on the hard stones. *Platter*-plat-plat-plat! It was not at all like soft grass!

"Where is the stable?" fretted the bigger lamb. "We must be going the wrong way." He could hear the wind in the roadside trees. *Shhhh, shhhhhhh!* it sighed. Shadows flickered and darted like live things. The big lamb jumped, skittering backwards on stiff legs. "There may be wolves about," he bleated, and he thought about the shepherds and the other sheep in the flock back on the safe hillside. "We were foolish to come so far," he scolded. "We are lost. I know we're lost. We won't be able to find the Child."

"Nothing is found unless it is looked for," said the little lamb. "I will look for the Baby. You go back to the other sheep."

And the big lamb hurried back the way they had come. He left the little lamb looking up at the stars. One star shone brighter than the rest. "The shepherds saw a bright light," the lamb remembered. "I will go to the place where that star is."

Over the fields he ran, leaving the road and the shadowy trees. Over tussocks of grass. Over low bushes, over rocks. Over low stone walls.

He came to a town. Dogs barked. The lamb's heart beat fast.

Platter-plat-plat-plat! He ran through a street, he ran past houses, he ran to an inn and on to a stable. Its door stood partly opened. The lamb stood still, looking inside.

The stable was lit by firelight.

A donkey's feet clinked on the stone floor.

A cow mooed softly.

A baby cried. The cry was no louder than a bleat of a newly-born lamb.

"Nothing is found unless it is searched for," said the lamb.

He trotted into the stable, knowing that he had found the Christ Child.

SLIT

CUT

A LAMB TO MAKE

If you have a tiny toy lamb he could stand in your crèche during Christmas, or you can make a lamb.

One way is to fold a small square of thin cardboard into two equal halves. A bigger person will draw the lamb's legs if you need help. Cut out the legs, using the drawing lines as a guide.

Now very carefully snip a *short* way along the crease you made in the cardboard. Just cut far enough to slip the lamb's head into the slit.

Make the head and long neck from another piece of cardboard. Push it into the slit and fasten it in firmly with sticky tape.

Tiny scraps of paper or wool clippings can be pasted all over the lamb's body to make fleece. Wool unravelled from knitting looks curly so you may be able to get hold of some of that.

The lamb's tail can be a snipping of wool or string. Glue that on. And he'll need eyes and a little black nose. Draw those on. Blacken his hoofs, too, if you want to. Now the lamb is finished.

Other animals can be made in a similar way and stand in the crèche with the lamb.

OLD DONKEY AND OX AND LITTLE GREY SHEEP

Animals watched Him
as He lay asleep . . .
old donkey and ox
and little grey sheep.
He lay in their hay
inside the feed-box
of the little old donkey,
grey sheep and the ox.
They shared their stable,
They gave what they could . . .
three farm animals
in a shed of wood.
They stood by drowsily
and He lay asleep . . .
old donkey and ox
and little grey sheep.

EAT WELL! SLEEP WELL!

In some countries it is often very cold at Christmas. Children especially remember the animals then. Farm animals are given extra food, often twice as much as usual, and they are told,

"Eat well! Sleep well!
This is Christmas Eve!"

Swedish children say that a friendly little gnome called a *tomte* helps to look after their animals. Finnish children know him as the *tonto*, and Danish children are just as sure the gnome is their *nisse*. He lives in a tiny secret place, perhaps in a tree, or under the floorboards of a barn, in a crack in a door, a hide-away corner in a room or under the roof. The nisse loves to eat creamy rice-pudding or porridge. A bowl filled to the brim is left for him to find on Christmas Eve. If the family cat finds it first and laps up the gift no one scolds greedy puss. "The nisse let the cat eat it," the children say, and another bowl of pudding is left for the gnome. The children watch for his pointed red cap to bob round a corner, but he's hard to catch sight of, so no one can be sure of seeing him.

You can make your own nisse as a finger-puppet gift, or to hang on a Christmas tree. A whole family of Nisse are called *Nissen*.

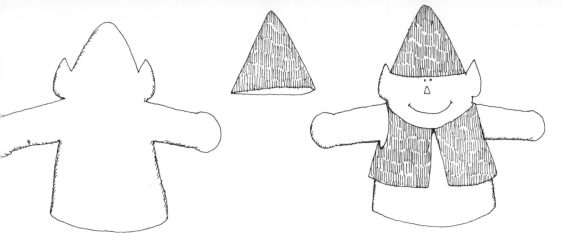

NISSE FINGER-PUPPET

Draw a pattern from the picture.

Now use the pattern to cut out two nisse shapes from grey felt, or other thick grey material. The nisse always wears grey clothes.

Glue or stitch the sides together, leaving the bottom free so that the nisse can fit over a finger.

The nisse always wears a red cap. Make that from the pattern using red material. Stitch the sides and put it on his head.

Give him eyes and a mouth. Use a pen to do that.

If you think he needs a waistcoat, make one from a scrap of bright cloth. It is cut in one piece with holes to fit his arms through.

Now the nisse can be a finger-puppet, a tree decoration, or maybe both. A nissen family could have a little tree for themselves. If there are any leftover scraps of red felt, cut them into plump apples to hang amongst the gnomes.

Children who know the nisse well say that he slips into houses on Christmas Eve to leave small gifts under pillows, or hidden under cushions and in other secret places. And to encourage him to come, holly and evergreens are hung about doorways.

41

IN-A-MINUTE PUPPETS

It takes hardly any time to turn an empty match-box into a puppet. You can draw or paint a face on the match-box, then slip it on a finger . . . and one puppet is made.

Match-boxes, along with other small boxes without ends, can become a family of puppets. Animals or people? You decide.

You can use all kinds of scraps to make their faces, and all kinds of scraps to make their clothes. Have you thought of using leaves, or corn husks?

Nick and Paul are brothers. How would you dress them for their rhyme?

Nick and Paul have long dancing legs and long stretching arms. You can cut each one from a long narrow piece of paper, creased into concertina folds. Begin the folds at one end. Crease the paper one way. Now turn it about and fold the paper the other way. Keep on with alternate folds until the paper is used. Glue it into place as a leg or an arm. Make three more limbs.

The puppets can wear floppy hats made in the same way if you like.

Two little puppets danced on a wall.
Dance the puppets
One was Nick,
Bend your finger to make Nick bow
One was Paul.
Make Paul bow
Nick danced off . . . *Woops!*
Hide Nick behind your back
So did Paul . . . *Wheee!*
Hide Paul behind your back
Then back came Nick,
Bring Nick back
And back came Paul.
Bring Paul back
Two little puppets danced on a wall.
Dance the puppets

STICKY-STICK PUPPETS

The next time you have an ice-cream or an ice-block on a thin flat stick, save it to make a stick puppet.

It only needs a face glued to one end and the puppet is ready for play.

Draw the face yourself or cut it from a magazine no one needs.

Ice-cream spoons can be turned into puppet dolls, too.

RINGS ON EACH FINGER

Ring puppets take a little longer to make because the paper rings must be made first. Cut some narrow strips of paper and glue each one into a circle, big enough to fit over a finger tip. Let each ring have a puppet face which you can draw or cut from a magazine, an old book or a newspaper. Glue or staple the face to a ring. Why not make a puppet for each finger? Ten puppets! Other puppets can be favourite story people, nursery-rhyme characters or someone no one has ever seen before because *you* invented him!

SHALL I TELL YOU?

Shall I tell you who will come
    to Bethlehem on Christmas Morn,
Who will kneel then gently down
    before the Lord, new-born?

One small fish from the river,
    with scales red, red gold,
One wild bee from the heather,
    one grey lamb from the fold,
One ox from the high pasture,
    one black bull from the herd,
One goatling from the far hills,
    one white, white bird.

And many children — God give them grace,
bringing tall candles to light Mary's face.

Shall I tell you who will come
    to Bethlehem on Christmas Morn,
Who will kneel then gently down
    before the Lord, new-born?

Ruth Sawyer

It is said by some people that birds and animals were given
the gift of speech on Christmas Eve. This is one of the stories
told about the birds, and particularly about a robin that lived
near Bethlehem.

ROBIN'S RED BREAST

A big black bird, the raven, had stayed out far too long. It was dark when he came flying back to his roost. The wind buffeted and pushed him about, forcing him to beat his wings strongly as he flew over the houses of Bethlehem.

He had hardly left the town behind him when suddenly the sky filled with light. It seemed brighter than starlight, brighter than moonlight. Below him the raven could clearly see sheep on a hillside, and a cornfield. He saw shepherds standing near a fire, staring upward into the sky behind the raven.

The bird swerved, turning about to look back at Bethlehem and the light. It was made by a star brighter than a thousand lanterns.

"The Christ Child has been born!" croaked the raven. "I must tell the other birds at once." He soared away, high in the air, flying fast to wake the wren.

"Wake up! Wake up, Wren!" shouted the raven. "Wake up! The Child is born. His star shines *now* in the sky!"

"I am awake. I can hear you," called the wren. "I will go to see the Baby at once. I'll take Him a blanket, softly woven from leaves and moss."

"And I will go and wake the cock," flustered the raven.

"Rooster! Rooster! Wake your hens!" shouted the raven. "The Child is born. I have seen His star."

Chu-chu-choooook! The rooster flapped and fussed. *Ch-chu-choooook!* His hens were already awake, clucking and crooning about him. "I must tell the world that the Babe is born," the rooster told them. *Pffft!* He puffed out his chest. "I shall say, *cock-a-doodle-doo! Cock-a-doo! No!* No, I will not. Cock-a-doodle does not sound important enough."

"What shall you say then?" clucked the hens.

"I shall crow. I shall crow in my most beautiful tones," said the rooster. "And I only have until dawn to practise. Listen now, hens, how is this?" And the rooster doodled and doodled and doodled.

At dawn he stood on a fence and his crowing was heard all over Bethlehem. *"Christus natus est!"* he shouted joyfully in the old language of Latin. It sounded important. His hens were proud and his hens were surprised. None of them had heard the rooster crow in anything but doodles before.

By then the raven had found the nightingale. Her voice was far sweeter than the rooster's, sweeter than any other bird's. She flew to the stable to sing to the Christ Child.

Other birds came flying to the stable. They came from trees, from the tall grass, from bushes and shrubs. Among them was a little brown robin, too small to be noticed and heartsick as he listened to the nightingale's song. He too had hoped to chirp his good-morning greeting to the Baby, but it would be dull music to hear after the nightingale's glorious song. He wished there was a way to show his joy and to give the Child a gift, but the robin could not fly strongly like the raven. He could not weave like the wren. He could not crow like the cock. He could not sing like the nightingale.

The robin hopped a little closer to the stable door. He saw the manger-bed was close to the fire. And he saw a flame suddenly leap higher than the rest. Would its heat redden the Baby's cheeks?

Swiftly the robin flew through the door, into the stable. With widely spread wings he fluttered between the fire and the Child's head. He hovered there, hardly moving. Faster and faster and faster beat his wings until they whirred like a fan. He stayed there until Mary lifted the Baby from His bed. By then, the robin's breast-feathers were scorched by the fire's heat.

And since that morning, every robin's breast is the colour of a bright flame. It may be scarlet-red, or orange, or yellow. Look for a robin and see for yourself.

BREAD AND MILK

Bread and milk for breakfast,
And woollen socks to wear,
And a crumb for Robin Red-breast
On the cold days of the year.

Christina Rossetti

REMEMBER THE BIRDS

Remember the birds at Christmas time, especially if you live where the weather is cold, or in a place where there aren't many trees.

In some countries farm children bunch wheat together and fasten it to a bird-pole in the yard — a high pole out of the reach of hunting cats.

Other children sprinkle seed on window-sills.

Birds like Christmas pudding, too. Their pudding is a little ball of fat, rolled in seeds and grated apple, and perhaps some crumbs. It can be hung near a window for the birds to find.

Half a coconut hung in a tree, or in another high place, will make a meal for a lot of birds. And don't forget to leave cake or breadcrumbs for them.

When it's hot, a bowl of water left in a safe place will bring birds to drink and to bathe.

BIRD TREE

A bird tree, or a bird mobile is quickly made.

Cut a lot of little bird shapes from coloured paper, or light cardboard.

Staple to each a long tail made from narrow streamers of cellophane paper. Gold or silver papers or flimsy tissues can be used too, if you like.

Add cellophane wings, or draw them on.

Give each bird two eyes, one on either side of its head. The eyes can be drawn, or else paste on tiny scraps of paper, sequins or beads.

Now the bird is ready to be hung from a small tree made from a bare branch. Sew a hanging thread to the bird's back. Paper-clips bent into S-shapes can be used as hangers.

A flock of different sized birds in bright Christmas colours can belong to your tree.

Perhaps you would like to display several birds in a doorway or a window. A mobile looks best if the hanging threads are of uneven lengths—some short, some long, hung in a bunch. Or the birds can be fastened to a coathanger.

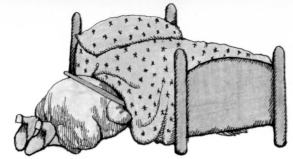

SILVERY SPIDERY TREE

Once there was a mother, and like mothers everywhere she worked to make her house spotlessly clean for Christmas.

Whisk, whisk, whisk! Her broom was all over the place. Into corners! Under the beds! Up over the ceilings! Down the walls! All over the place!

After that, her duster went everywhere. *Flick, flick, flick!* It gathered up dust. It gathered up fluff. *Flick-flick-flick!*

The spiders who lived in the house had a dreadful time with the chasings from the broom and the duster. Skittle-skattle, off they scuttled double-quick, running to hide goodness-knows-where. And so those little grey furry spiders never saw the Christmas tree.

Just before Christmas, when the children were asleep, the tree was brought into the sitting-room and stood near the window.

On Christmas Eve, the mother hung the tree with decorations which she kept from one Christmas to the next. On the branches went tiny toys and glittery ornaments and gilded-goldy walnuts, and stiff little white candles. After all was done, the mother shut the door into the sitting-room very firmly. *No one* must see the tree before Christmas morning. And it was no use children trying to peep, or begging-or-nagging-or-asking-or-demanding-or-crying to see the tree. No! The tree was a surprise.

However, the animals who lived in the house always managed to see the tree before the children did on Christmas morning. It was easy for them. First, the cat! She sidled in

when the mother went in to draw back the curtains.

Then the dog trotted in when the mother carried the presents to put under the tree.

And the canary? His cage hung in the sitting-room window. He knew everything there was to know about the tree. Even a mouse who lived secretly somewhere or other, scampered out to look at the tree.

Only the furry spiders—the fat mother spiders and the fat father spiders and the little teeny tiny tonky baby spiders, had never seen the tree. They did not dare to leave their hiding-holes, yet how they longed to see it, just once!

Then, one Christmas Eve, they made up their minds that they would.

When no one was looking, because the mother was asleep and so were her children, and so were the cat, the dog, and the canary, the spiders came creepy-crawling up the stairs from the bottom of the house. They came creepy-crawling down the stairs from the top of the house. They came creepy-crawling along the hallway. And they went creepy-crawling under the sitting-room door across the floor to where the tree stood.

Fat mother spiders and fat father spiders and all the little teeny tiny tonky baby spiders went creepy-crawling round the tree. Round and round and round looking at its loveliness!

And when they had seen everything they could see from the floor, the fat mother spiders and the fat father spiders and the little teeny tiny tonky baby spiders went creepy-crawling up the trunk of the tree into the branches. Round

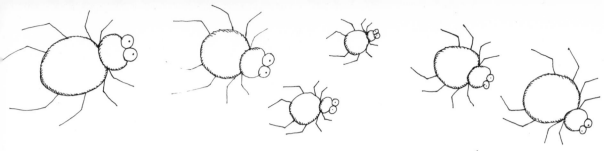

and round and round! Higher and higher to the top! Looking and seeing, looking and seeing!

They saw the tiny gay toys, every glittery ornament, all the gilded-goldy walnuts and each stiff little white candle. In and out of the branches! Round and round! Up and down! Creepy-crawling everywhere!

When there was nothing more to be seen the fat mother spiders and the fat father spiders and the little teeny tiny tonky baby spiders scuttled back to their hiding-holes. They left the tree covered in cobwebs, fine threads of cobwebs.

Christmas morning came.

The children of the house burst into the sitting-room. *"Oooooh!"* they said. They stopped in their tracks. Their hands flew to their faces. They stared at the tree. They drew in their breaths. "OH!"

The mother of the house followed behind them. "Oh, my goodness!" she cried out. "Oh my goodness!"

Never had they seen anything like their tree. Beautiful! Silvered! A shimmering, glittering tree! From top to bottom it sparkled with tinsel, tinsel as fine as angels' hair, as fine as the gossamer threads of cobwebs.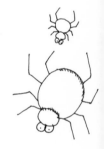

And no one knew, not the canary bird who had slept all night, not the mother and not the children, that the tinselled webs silvering the tree had been left by the little grey furry spiders. The fat mother spiders and the fat father spiders and the little teeny tiny tonky baby spiders had been glad to share the tree.

TREES TO MAKE

You can make a tree for someone from one of these ideas.
Most of them you can make alone without help.

Silvery tree

You don't need families of spiders to
make a silvery tree, just lots of tinsel.
Wrap it round and round a little tree,
or a bare branch, until it shimmers and
glitters and glistens. Top the tree with
a bright bauble. If it stands in a tin or a
flower-pot filled with sand, cover the
pot with kitchen foil.

Matchstick tree

For a matchstick tree find lots of used
matches. Glue them into a spiky tree
shape. Sprinkle the tree with glue, then
glitter, or paint it. Another way to
decorate it is to drip the wax from
lighted birthday candles over the tree.
A grown-up can help you do that.

Bare Branch tree

One of the loveliest little trees is just a
bare branch painted white and stuck in

a pot filled with sand. Decorate the tree any way you like. You may like to hang it with baubles or stars, or red and purple hearts cut from felt or cardboard. Danish children cut plump little apples from thin pine wood. Balsa wood is easy to cut. Paint each apple red with vegetable dye and give it two little green leaves. Or hang lots of foil-covered sweets like parcels on the branches. Snip them off for the visitors to your house.

Cone tree
A cone tree can be decorated in your own way too. First, make the cone from a circle of cardboard. Fasten it together with sticky tape, then trim the bottom so that it stands straight. Now paint it in stripes, squiggles and curls, or decorate it with paper cut-outs, or strings of paper dolls. Rows and rows of braid and lace are another way to trim it. Find a way that suits you best and finish off the tree with a star on the top, or a bauble.

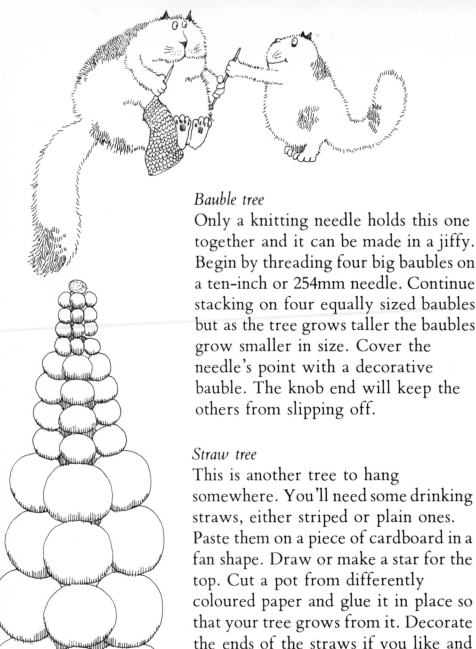

Bauble tree

Only a knitting needle holds this one together and it can be made in a jiffy. Begin by threading four big baubles on a ten-inch or 254mm needle. Continue stacking on four equally sized baubles but as the tree grows taller the baubles grow smaller in size. Cover the needle's point with a decorative bauble. The knob end will keep the others from slipping off.

Straw tree

This is another tree to hang somewhere. You'll need some drinking straws, either striped or plain ones. Paste them on a piece of cardboard in a fan shape. Draw or make a star for the top. Cut a pot from differently coloured paper and glue it in place so that your tree grows from it. Decorate the ends of the straws if you like and add a string to hang the tree.

Macaroni tree

Macaroni comes in many shapes, including shells and stars. Decide which shapes you want to use and make them into a tree pattern. Glue into place. Your tree will look most handsome if it is glued on to coloured cardboard. The macaroni can be painted gold, or another colour. Rice and other seeds can be used to make tree shapes, too.

A tree to eat

Dip an ice-cream cone into some icing, then roll it in coconut. Put a cherry on top.

Another way is to trim the iced tree with cherries and silver cake-decorating balls. Tiny sweets are yet another idea.

And still another way is to thread popcorn on string and wind it round the tree. But don't eat the string later on!

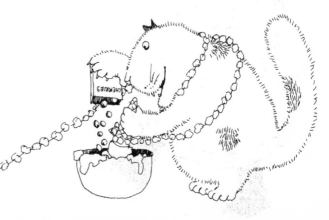

Lemon tree
A tree for grown-ups. Cover fruit with squares of plastic film from the kitchen. Pull each covering free of wrinkles and twist the ends to seal off air. Stack into a tree shape. It will be self-supporting. Finish off with a few ivy leaves tucked between the lemons. Faded leaves can be renewed. The fruit should remain fresh for about three weeks even in the hot summer.
Oranges can be used instead of lemons, or the tiny tart Christmas apples, or little golden cumquats.

Children who live in Sweden don't worry if it's freezing cold during Christmas. They sally outside to dance about a tree, singing the *Ritsch, Ratsch* nonsense song and other rollicking Christmas carols. Their cheeks glow and soon they feel warm all over.

RITSCH, RATSCH, FILIBOM!

Ritsch, ratsch filibom bom bom,
Filibom bom bom,
Filibom bom bom!
Ritsch, ratsch filibom bom bom,
Filibom bom bom,
Filibom!

CHRISTMAS IN TWO LANDS

There it is cold, or there is snow —
And holly, fires and mistletoe,
And carols sung out in the street
By children, walking through the sleet.
Church bells break the frozen air
Ringing loudly everywhere.
There is where white winter glory
Comes to tell the Christmas story.

Here it is hot, the sun is gold —
And turns tired when day is old,
Christmas carols are sung at night
Somewhere outside, by candle-light.
Church bells ring out in the heat
And call to people in the street.
The Christmas story here is told
In summer, when the sun is gold.

Joan Mellings

THE LITTLE JUGGLER OF CHARTRES

One, two, three, then four, then five, then *six* balls of brightly polished copper flew into the air, to spin above the boy's head in a whirring circle, then another circle, and another. Higher and faster spun the balls. The crowd watching the little juggler shouted and clapped, enjoying the skill of his small thin hands.

Then the boy failed to catch a ball. It fell and the rhythm of his juggling was broken. The other balls clattered to the cobblestones, rolling everywhere. He crawled after them, gathered them up and began to juggle again. Once more he missed a ball. Again they all clattered to the ground. When it happened for the third time, the crowd jeered, then drifted away to their business in the market place of Chartres.

Alone now, the boy tried to recover his skill, but he was almost too weak from hunger and a fever to hold the heavy balls of copper. Then he slipped himself and fell to lie like a crumpled heap of rags. He was too sick to move or to cry out when someone pushed him under a bench, along with a bag of turnips.

An hour or so later, when Brother Boniface crossed the square from the cathedral, the little juggler was still lying there. The priest almost mistook the lad for a bag of turnips as he loaded his little handcart. "Who is this boy?" he asked. "Just a juggler from somewhere," he was told. No one knew or cared. "The lad is ill," mumbled Brother Boniface. "Then you can have him," someone else told him.

60

And Brother Boniface took the boy as if he weighed no more than a goose and propped him carefully amongst the turnips and cabbages, the onions and eggs and a brace of chickens. Then he trundled his cart back to the cathedral and his kitchen.

There the little juggler was wrapped in a blanket and fed a herbal tea, followed by broth.

It was weeks before the little juggler was nursed back to health, and as he had nowhere to go, he stayed with the monks at the cathedral. Most of the time he helped Brother Boniface with his work. There were vegetables to prepare, stew-pans to scrub and platters to clean. At no time did he juggle with the six balls of heavy copper. They were wrapped in a parcel of cloth and left to tarnish on a kitchen shelf. It was as if they were forgotten, along with the boy's old life when he had moved from market town to market town, juggling for pennies to buy his bread. Too often he had been hungry, too often he had been cold.

He was content until the coming of Christmas, with its short grey days and falls of snow. The boy watched the monks, all busy with their preparations to celebrate the birth of Our Lord. He spoke to Brother Boniface about it as he stirred a vegetable stew one morning. "Yesterday I watched the painting brother making a new picture to hang in Our Lady's Chapel," he said. "And I have heard the singing monk making a new song of praise for Christmas."

"And have you seen Brother Francis' carvings?" asked Brother Boniface. "He is making a new font for the chapel."

"Yes, I have seen it and I have looked at the new book which the writing monk is making. Brother Boniface, what can I do to help celebrate the birth of Jesus?"

"You, my lad, can cut the vegetables so perfectly that none is wasted," Brother Boniface told the boy. "You can make a soup so delicious, with pearls of onions and bouquets of herbs, that no cook could better it. You can fill the stomachs of our monks to give them the strength and warmth they need to do their best work."

"But that is doing very little and it is what I do each day," said the boy.

"And so it is," agreed Brother Boniface. "Each must do what he does best. So together we shall make some honey cakes for the Christmas feast."

When the time came to make the honey cakes, however, the little juggler was missing from the kitchen. "He must be away gathering herbs in the fields, or helping the gardening monks," decided Brother Boniface.

But the boy was neither in the fields, nor the vegetable gardens; he was crouched before the statue of Our Lady in her little chapel. He was unwrapping the cloth parcel holding the six balls of copper, and then he polished each one until it glistened.

Kneeling on one leg, he tossed a ball high . . . then two . . . three balls spun higher . . . four . . . five, . . . *six* whirred in growing circles before the statue of Our Lady!

I CAN'T JUGGLE CAN YOU ?

His fingers were stiff at first, but in no time their old skill returned. And the boy sang as he juggled the glinting balls.

Each day he came to the chapel and performed in front of the statue, and when he had finished juggling he knelt to pray his thanks for his deft hands with the copper balls.

A monk, coming to clean the tall brass candlesticks in Our Lady's Chapel, heard the little juggler singing. But his smiles faded in anger when he saw that the boy was juggling. The monk hurried from the chapel calling for the other monks and the abbot himself to deal with the boy. "This is an outrage! The boy must be stopped. Our Lady's Chapel is not a fairground!" the monk told the others.

Fascinated and shocked, they watched the boy. The Abbot came. Brother Boniface came. Then before anyone could speak, the little juggler dropped on his knees before the statue. "Holy Mother," he said, "Please accept my juggling which I have done in your honour."

The monks were astonished to see the lips of the statue curl into a smile; no longer cold marble, Our Lady stretched across and blessed the boy.

"A miracle! This is a miracle!" whispered the monks; and even as they spoke the statue was again marble.

After that, the little juggler often performed before the statue of Our Lady. No one interfered. The boy had offered what he could do best during that Christmas at Chartres.

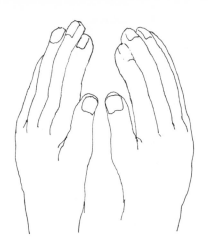
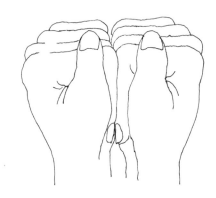

Many people go to church on Christmas morning.
Here is an old finger game about people in church.

THIS IS THE CHURCH

This is the church
Put your palms together. Tuck your fingers into fists so that finger nails are touching.

And this is the steeple
Bring out the two pointing fingers and let them meet at their tips. That makes the steeple.

Open the door
Open out your thumbs like a door opening.

And there are the people
Turn your hands over and waggle your finger people.

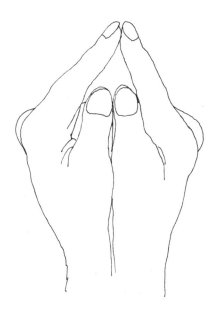
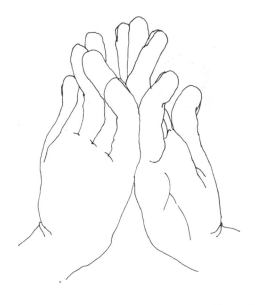

CATCH THE BELL-RINGER

A bumping game to play outdoors! On a lawn or in a wide clear space is the best place. Someone older is needed to watch that the players don't collide too hard.

All the players except the bell-ringer are blindfolded. The bell-ringer dodges about them ringing his bell *non-stop*.

The others try to catch him by following the tinkling sound.

If you don't have a bell, put some little stones into a tin and fasten the lid tightly.

No one must run. Walking is the rule. Out go the runners! No more play for them just now. Everyone walks very fast, trying to catch the bell-ringer. Whoever does that becomes the new bell-ringer and the game begins all over again.

WHO REMEMBERED JOANNA?

In a paddock, amongst tall weeds and long straggling grass stood a little stone church. It had a wooden steeple, and in the steeple hung one bell. It was called Joanna, but no one remembered why.

Ding dong! Ding dong! Once each month the bell rang out over the paddocks. Old Mr Patrick had walked from his farm to pull Joanna's bell rope. Up, down he pulled. *Ding dong!* Joanna swung to and fro and the heavy clapper struck the side of the bell. *Ding dong!*

Soon afterwards the parson drove out from town to the little church in the paddock. And Aunt Stella came on her bike to play the organ. And people came from their farms to take part in the morning service.

Ding dong! Ding dong! Old Mr Patrick and Joanna hurried along the latecomers.

Nicky always liked his family to be at church early. Then he had time to run round to the church tower and watch Mr Patrick ring Joanna. Up and down, up and down, he pulled the rope. To and fro swayed Joanna. DING DONG! she shouted. That's how loudly her voice sounded inside the bell tower. Mr Patrick and Nicky could not hear each other speak.

When Christmas came, Joanna was to ring for a special service at nine o'clock in the morning. Nicky's mother went to church long before then. She went very early before it was hot. She took an armful of flowers from her garden to decorate the church: pink roses, blue hydrangeas and big white daisies.

Nick helped her to carry the flowers from the car. Then he helped her to fill the tall brass vases with water from the tank at the back of the church. By the time his mother had finished arranging the flowers, the church had filled with bright sunlight. Everything looked polished and cheerful, as if it were waiting. "All we need now is for Joanna to ring," said Nick.

"Oh, Joanna!" said his mother. "I had forgotten the bell."
Nicky looked puzzled. "Forgotten?"

"Don't you know, Nicky, Mr Patrick has hurt his arm." his mother told him. "He won't be able to ring the bell."

"We could ring Joanna," said Nicky.

"Could we!" his mother sounded surprised, then she said: "Well, we could try. There isn't time to bring someone who is a proper bell-ringer."

They hurried to the tower. There was Joanna's rope hanging limply. Nick's mother took hold of it in both hands. She pulled. "Oooh!" She hadn't expected the bell to feel so heavy. *"Clong!"* said Joanna sulkily, as if she'd expected a firmer, stronger yank on her rope.

"I'll help you pull," offered Nick. "I know how to do it."

He stood in front of his mother and they both tugged on the rope. *C-c-c-clangggg!* shuddered Joanna. Her voice was not right.

"She should ding-dong," said Nicky.

"I don't think we were pulling at exactly the same time," said his mother. "Perhaps that is the trouble."

"Let's count so that we can," said Nick.

"Right! We'll count one-two. On the two we'll pull down very hard. Ready now?"

"Ready!" said Nick.

"One . . . *two!*" they counted. And they pu*lll*ed. "One . . . *two!*" they pu*lll*ed.

Ding . . . dong!

Across the paddocks on his farmhouse verandah old Mr Patrick listened to Joanna. He nodded and he smiled and he wondered who had set her ringing so well. "Who remembered Joanna?" he said aloud. "I wonder if it was Nicky? Oh no, it couldn't have been Nick. He's not big enough to pull the bell rope."

But later that day, Mr Patrick knew that it *was* Nicky who had rung Joanna, with his mother to help.

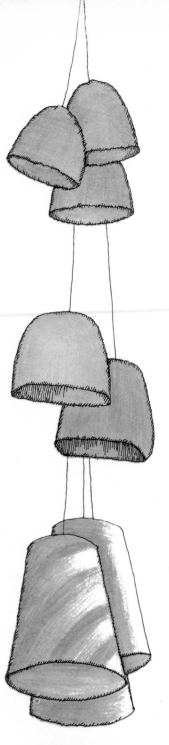

BELLS TO MAKE

Little tinkling bells are quickly made from lots of metallic milk or cream bottle-tops. Press each one over the peak of a lemon squeezer to make a bell shape.

Now thread the bells into bunches. *Shake-shake! Tinkle-tinkle-tinkle!*

Bunches of little bells can glitter from the branches of a Christmas tree, or they can hang in doorways to sway in a breeze.

Small bells can be made from the cups of egg cartons. Tear or cut them from a carton, then paint each one, or cover in kitchen foil or bright paper. Hang the bells in pairs.

Bigger bells can be made from paper cups. Cover these with kitchen foil too. You may like to hang them in threes.

Try making a string of bells.
Fold some paper in half—any paper, even newspaper.
Fold it again. Fold it *again*, then once more.
Draw half a bell down one crease.

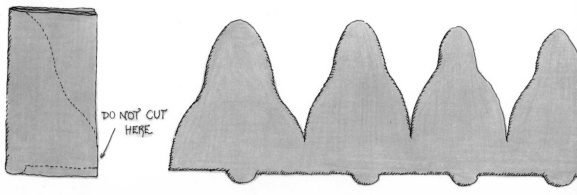

DO NOT CUT HERE

Cut out the bell shape as shown in the picture.
Unfold the paper—and there's a string of bells!

Another way to make little bells is to cut out circles of paper. Perhaps you could use a saucer as a guide to make a neat circle.
Fold the paper in halves, then fold it again to divide the circle into four parts.
Cut along each crease. Now you have four pieces of paper. Roll each one into a bell shape. Fasten it together with sticky tape or glue.
Sew a thread to the top, ready to hang the bell.

If you make popcorn, don't butter and salt all of it. Put some aside to soften a little. Then it can be easily threaded on thin wire. The wire can be pushed into a bell shape. (Into other shapes too . . . stars, leaves, icicles, dancing figures, anything you like.) Fasten the wire off firmly by twining it over itself. Leave a loose end to make a hook, and your popcorn ornament is ready as a parcel or tree decoration.

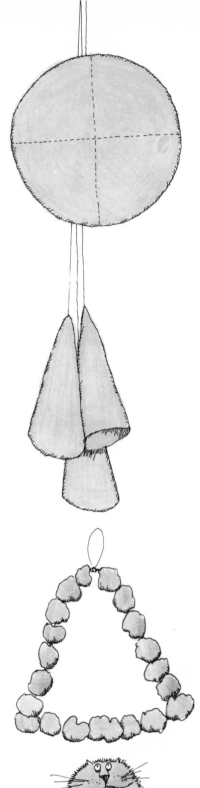

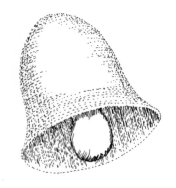

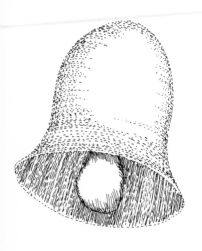

Margaret's sugar bells glisten as if covered in frost. To make them, mix enough egg white with sugar to turn the mixture into crumbles.

Into that goes a few drops of vanilla or almond essence and some food colouring. Stir it well until the colour is evenly spread through the sugar crumbs. Grease the insides of some egg cups, or plastic bells if you have any. Fill them with the sugar mixture, pressing it firmly down into each mould.

Now is the time to be patient. Put them aside until the sugar mixture hardens. Don't touch! Don't fiddle! Let it dry for at least another day. It may take a week for bigger bells, as the sugar forms a deceptively hard crust on the outside.

Once the bells have hardened, some sugar can be scooped out to leave a shell inside the mould.

Tap the bells free from the mould and give each one a fat round clapper made from rolled silver paper.

The bells can be used to decorate a Christmas cake. Later on, someone may like to eat one or two.

WELCOME

Welcome to our house!
We have gifts for you.
Big red apples, round and juicy,
Brown Brazil nuts and some sweeties.
Then we'll sing our songs,
Christmas songs for you.

THE WAY OF WISHES

A long time ago it was, and late on Christmas Eve when Farmer Goody and his wife were wakened by a pounding and a thumping on their kitchen door. Two strangers were there, asking for food and shelter for the night.

"Come in! Come in at once!" said Farmer Goody. "Rest yourselves by the fire."

"Tomorrow is Christmas," said Mrs Goody, giving them bowls of soup. "You must stay and share our Christmas feast."

The travellers were glad to stay.

The next morning they went with the Goody family to church. There was quite a crowd of them, for the Goody household included lots of children.

Then it was home again to dinner. The children sat close together on a long bench to make room for the two travellers at the table. As far as Christmas dinners go, it didn't seem to be very grand, but it was the best the farm could offer. There was hot roast meat and potatoes, then a big bowl of creamy rice-pudding. The Goody family all ate a little less so that there was plenty for the travellers' plates.

After the meal there was so much laughter and talking and singing that the travellers didn't leave until the next morning. "I'm glad you stayed," said Farmer Goody. "It is a pity that you won't be with us next Christmas."

"We'll do our best to get here," said the travellers. "Thank you, Mrs Goody, we won't forget your good cooking. How many dishes did you serve?"

"Roast meat with potatoes, then creamy rice-pudding," she said. "Just the two."

"Then we'll grant you two wishes," said one traveller.

"What do you want more than anything in the world?" asked the second.

"That's easy to decide," said Mrs Goody. "All we need is food enough to feed our children, and happiness and peace."

"Your wishes will be granted," promised the travellers.

They were, too. From that day the farm prospered. The cow had twin calves. The sheep had twin lambs. The pig had so many baby piglets it was hard to count them. And the crops grew better than weeds. Soon people from far and near, were talking about the Goody family's fortune.

"It all began when two strangers stayed with us at Christmas time," Mrs Goody said. "We hope they will visit us again this coming Christmas. I'll cook a perfect dinner for them then. One to remember. I'll have roast duck and roast pork, cold ham and hot plum pudding, bowls of raisins. . ."

When Farmer Slybones heard the story he told Mrs Goody, "I do believe your guests were the very same strangers we turned away from our house last year. We feel very badly about it, being Christmas and all. So promise me, Mrs Goody, that you'll send them to my farm when they turn up again."

I LOVE BABY PIGLETS AND RICE-PUDDING!

"Of course, I will," beamed Mrs Goody. "I can see that you want to make it up to them because you sent them away."

And so, when Christmas came again Mrs Goody sent the travellers to Slybones' Farm, soon after they had arrived at her house. "We'll be back in the morning to go to church with you," they promised as they left.

The Slybones had an enormous feast waiting for the travellers. There was ham and bacon. Hot mashed potatoes, cold potato salads, baked potatoes oozing with cheese, and crisp fried potatoes. Long sausages, thin sausages, fat sausages! Juicy pies and hot breads, sliced beetroots and pickled cabbage. There was a big pudding. There were cakes and buns, creamy custards and sweets and nuts and plenty to drink.

It was very late before the travellers could go to bed.

They slept on soft mattresses, under silken sheets and rested their heads on featherdown pillows.

On Christmas morning they rose early to go to church with the Goody family. "I can't allow you to walk all that way," objected Farmer Slybones. "You must take our horses. Ride to church!" He kept urging the travellers to ride to church and almost missed hearing their goodbyes. Mrs Slybones tugged at his elbow, and he heard her hissing, "They haven't asked us how many dishes we ate last night."

Oh-oh-oh! The travellers were now mounting the horses, but before Slybones had time to be disappointed one of them was calling out, "That was a magnificent meal last night, Mrs Slybones. Our thanks for it. Tell me now, how many dishes did you serve?"

76

"Well, let me see . . ." she began putting up her fingers to count them. Slybones quickly pushed her hand away and said quickly, "Too many for her to count."

"If that is the case, then we'll grant you four wishes," said the traveller. "Two wishes for yourself and two for your wife."

Well! Before the travellers had gone down the road the Slybones were quarrelling about the best way to spend the four wishes. She wanted silk and velvet gowns. He wanted more milking cows. She wanted gold bracelets and pearl earrings. He wanted the biggest farm thereabouts. She wanted fur slippers. He wanted . . . oh, there was no end to their wants.

Farmer Slybones became so annoyed he stamped out of the house to do some ploughing. His bad temper brought him more trouble. He was so busy thinking about his wife's silly wishes and wondering how he could make her spend her wishes in *his* way that he drove the horses and plough into a fence. "Stupid horses!" he shouted. "Look where you're going! I wish I didn't have to worry about you or the plough!"

Whisk! The horses vanished. The plough vanished. Just disappeared into the air. Gone for ever! Slybones stood alone in the field with his first wish wasted.

Grumbling and growling, he trudged towards his house. Little did he know that his wife was waiting for him at the farmhouse door. She looked this way, that way and then over the fields. "Where did Slybones get to? He's nowhere to be seen," she fretted. "We could use our wishes at once if he were only here. I wish he was here, right beside me now."

Whizz! And there he was beside her on the doorstep. Mrs Slybones had wasted the second wish, and a noisy argument followed. A shouting, snarling, yelling, roaring, bad-mannered wrangle. Each blamed the other for wasting a wish. He shook his fist. She stamped her feet. The row must have been heard all over the countryside. It was a snip-snap brangle-jangle! Mrs Slybones was so mad she grabbed a plate holding the remains of the Christmas pudding. "I wish this was on the top of your head!" she screamed.

Squish! The pudding flew off the plate. *Slosh!* It flopped on to Slybones' head. A sprig of holly stuck out of the top. *Slurp!* Soft pudding and brandy sauce slithered into Slybones ears and eyes. A cherry wobbled to the end of his nose and stuck there.

"Help me! Help me!" he spluttered.

"How? What can I do?" cried his wife.

"Pull the pudding off."

"It won't come off!" She tried to spoon it off his head, but the pudding stayed stuck.

AREN'T THEY SILLY!

"Then wash it off."

"It won't wash off!" She threw a bucket of water over his head, but still the pudding stayed stuck.

"Then cut it off."

"It won't cut off!" She hacked at the pudding with a knife, but it still stuck.

"Then knock it off."

"It won't knock off!" She hit the pudding with her rolling-pin. Slybones spun across the room and the pudding stayed stuck just as fast.

"Oh, I wish you'd never made such a soggy pudding," roared Slybones.

Gerlup! Off came the pudding. Away it went to goodness-knows-where. Not a crumb was ever seen again. The brandy sauce went with it. So did the cherry from the end of Slybones' nose. And that was the last wish used up. What happened after that no one knows, because the story ends here.

IF WISHES WERE HORSES

If wishes were horses
Beggars would ride.

If turnips were watches
I'd wear one by my side.

If wishes were fishes
We'd serve them in dishes.

LUCKY WISHBONES

Do you save the wishbone when the family has chicken to eat? If you save them all through the year, you can give them away as lucky Christmas presents. First dry the wishbones so that they are hard and brittle. Then paint them gold or silver. Use them as decorations for the Christmas table, putting one beside each plate, or you can slip them inside bon-bons or crackers. Pull a wishbone with someone else, each of you taking hold of one end with your little finger. Snap! Whichever of you is left with the blade where the wishbone is joined can make a wish. Sssh! Don't tell anyone else what you have wished.

WISHING HARP

Next time there's chicken for dinner ask if you may have the wishbone. Use it to make a wishing harp.

Scrub the bone clean, then paint it if you like.

Fasten a rubber band across the opening. If the bone is small and fine the band will need to be twisted several times about it.

Pluck the harp with your fingers for a tiny twanging sound.

A bow of narrow ribbon could be tied to one end.

You could make several of these as good-luck presents for friends.

STAR-LIGHT, STAR-BRIGHT

Star-light, star-bright,
First star I've seen tonight.
I wish I may, I wish I might
Get the wish I wish tonight.

Some people say that for wishes to come true it's not enough to wish on the first star to shine in the night sky. For *seven* nights wishes must be made on the first seven stars to appear in the sky, then the wish might come true.

WASH THE DISHES

Wash the dishes,
Wipe the dishes,
Ring the bell for tea.
Three good wishes, three good kisses,
I will give to thee.

PARCEL

When I have a parcel —
Whether it's thick or it's thin,
When I have a parcel —
Whether it's round or it's square,
    Someone says,
"Hey! Stop peeping! Don't you dare!"
    So . . .
I just feel it
        and feel it
Then shake it a little,
And wonder
    and
        wonder
What's under the paper.
It's my parcel for Christmas —
I'll open it then,
Just as soon as I can
Get rid of that string!

JULKLAPP!

There were new neighbours in Elizabeth's street. There was a mother and a father and a little girl named Tina. She was six. When Tina was very little her family had lived in Germany. Now she lived in Australia, next door to Elizabeth.

On Christmas Eve, Elizabeth went with her parents to visit their new neighbours. They wanted to wish them a happy Christmas.

Elizabeth took a chocolate Santa Claus for Tina. It was wrapped in red-and-silver paper. She had another parcel, too, wrapped in white paper with a sprig of pink Christmas Bush flowers fastened to the top. Inside the paper was a thick slice of her mother's Christmas cake. Elizabeth knew how good it tasted. She had watched her mother make the cake with lots of fruits and nuts and cherries, then cover it with a white sugar frosting.

"Come in and welcome! Christmas happiness to you!" called Tina's mother, opening her front door even before they had reached it. "This pretty parcel can't be for me!" she laughed happily when Elizabeth handed her the cake. Then she kissed Elizabeth on both cheeks and the top of her head, saying, "Shoo, into the sitting-room with you, little one!"

The grown-ups seemed to be talking and laughing all at the same time, and Elizabeth went into the sitting-room as she'd been told.

And there was Tina's Christmas tree standing on a little table. From the lowest branches to the highest it was covered with decorations, so many decorations that it was hard to see any green tree at all. Tina's tree was hung with little red apples, silver bells and golden trumpets, red candles and white candles and lots of other things in different shapes. Elizabeth wasn't sure what they were until she stepped nearer to the tree to look more closely. Were they biscuits?

"Do you like our tree?" Tina's mother asked from behind her.

"Oh, yes!" said Elizabeth. "I just love it."

"Some of the things on it we brought with us from Germany," said Tina's mother. "But Tina and I make new biscuits each year to hang on the tree."

So they were biscuits.

"You may eat one later, but right now, would you like a sweet from the bowl under the tree?" Tina's mother was saying.

But Elizabeth had turned back to the tree to look at the biscuits hanging there. She saw fat little men biscuits, ring-a-ling bell biscuits, spiky fir-tree biscuits, flying-bird biscuits, round flower biscuits, pointed star biscuits, tall candle biscuits, striped drum biscuits. So many! And each one bright with cherries or nuts or silver sweets.

"Have something from each bowl," Tina's mother was telling Elizabeth now.

There were three bowls under the tree. One held sweets. One held nuts. One held apples, little red apples. And Tina's mother was pressing the rosiest apple into Elizabeth's hand. It felt round and smooth and it looked too good to eat. Elizabeth wanted to keep it. "Thank you," she said, "but where is Tina? Why isn't Tina here?"

The grown-ups were talking and laughing and crowding about the tree. Tina's mother hadn't heard her question. Elizabeth asked more loudly, "Please, where is Tina?" No one answered.

It was strange to be in a room full of people looking at Tina's tree, in Tina's house, yet she wasn't there. "I'll go and look for her," she decided.

Elizabeth moved towards the closed door. She was halfway across the carpet when the sitting-room door flew open. Something hurtled into the room. Someone shouted very loudly, *"Julklapp!"* Something landed at Elizabeth's feet. "Oooooh!" she said. "What's happening?"

A big parcel had been tossed into the room and Tina came skipping and chuckling behind it.

"A-ahhh!" Tina's mother was saying and clapping her hands together. "Elizabeth is the lucky one! The Julklapp parcel is for her."

"Yes, yes!" danced Tina. "See, there's your name on it. Elizabeth, it says. That writing says 'Elizabeth'. Take the paper off quickly now!" She was jumping about, not able to keep still and sending secret smiles across the room to her mother.

Elizabeth slipped off the string. What could be inside such a big fat soft parcel? She unwrapped some paper. It was longer than her arm. And under it was more paper and more string. Off that came. "This is a funny parcel," she said.

"It's a julklapp parcel. A surprise Christmas parcel in our old country," laughed Tina's mother. "What have you found, Elizabeth?"

"More paper!" she said.

And there was more paper, and more paper, and more and more and *more!*

"I don't think this parcel will ever end," Elizabeth laughed.

"Keep going!" Tina told her. "It's a julklapp parcel."

"At least it's getting smaller, that's something," said Tina's mother. "Keep going, Elizabeth!"

Elizabeth kept unwrapping the parcel. It did grow quite small. The pile of paper about her grew bigger and bigger. Soon the julklapp parcel was just big enough to fit in her hand. No bigger! Off came the last red paper. Now Elizabeth was holding a little white box. Silver stars had been stuck over the lid. "Oh, it is pretty!" she said.

"Look inside! Open the box!" Tina was telling her. She was standing so close to Elizabeth nothing could have fitted between them. The lid was lifted. Inside, on a white paper doily lay a fat little biscuit man. His eyes were currants and his nose was a blob of cherry. Down a coat of chocolate were five green button-sweets. "I love him!" said Elizabeth.

"I made him," said Tina. "You can eat him."

"He's too nice," said Elizabeth. "I'll keep him."

"You could put him on your Christmas tree," said Tina's mother. "We made a little hole in his cap. You can hang him by that."

"So I can," said Elizabeth. "Yes, I'll put him on our tree."

Then she remembered to give Tina her red-and-silver parcel. Inside was . . . the chocolate Santa Claus!

"He's too nice to eat too," said Tina. "Thank you, Elizabeth!"

And, do you know, there was a loop of silver string in the top of Santa's cap. Before anyone could say *julklapp* he was hanging on Tina's tree, right in the front for everyone to see.

Goodness knows if he was ever eaten, or Elizabeth's fat little biscuit man either.

PLAY DOUGH

Play dough makes biscuits which are *not* to be eaten but can be pretty enough to hang on a Christmas tree.

1 cup of plain flour
½ cup of cooking salt
About ½ cup of water
A little vegetable oil

Mix everything together into a firm dough. Roll out on a floured board. Cut into shapes. Put a piece of macaroni in the top of each shape. It will leave a hole to take a piece of string after the dough is baked.

Bake in a slow over at 225° until the biscuits are hard.

Decorate with paint with a little glue added to it: this will prevent the paint flaking off.

The biscuits can be decorated with tinsel, ribbons, braids, paper stars, lace, beads, or anything else you like to use.

The same dough can be plaited or curled or rolled into pretzel shapes. And it can make a gingerbread house.

If you don't want to paint your biscuits, cover them with glittery or coloured paper.

DECORATIONS TO MAKE

Invent your own shapes, or use some of these as a pattern guide.

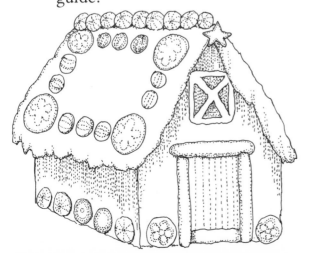

THE GINGERBREAD MAN

Smiling girls, rosy boys,
Come and buy my little toys!
Monkeys made from gingerbread
And sugar horses painted red!

WALNUTS AND MATCHES

At Christmas time there's special food to eat. Perhaps nuts in their shells come your way. Walnuts can be carefully cracked into two halves. After the nut kernel is eaten the shells can be floated as little boats.

You'll need a lump of play-dough or plasticine in the bottom of each shell. It will anchor down a match-stick mast.

Thread a piece of coloured paper through the match-stick to become a sail. Gold paper looks grand but you may like to use striped or patterned paper.

Why not make three ships? And let them sail away as presents for someone you like.

90

THE PARTY

Tony went to the zoo. He saw the bears and the tiger, the giraffe and the monkeys. "I hope to see you again soon," he called to them as he was leaving.

And so, on Monday, the biggest bear came to Tony's house.

He knocked on the front door. Rat-a-tat-tat! He growled. But Tony wasn't there. He was at his Grandma's house helping to make Christmas cakes. So the bear went away.

On Tuesday he was back again. The middle-sized bear came too. They knocked on the front door. Tap-a-tap-tap! They knocked on the back door. Rap-a-rap-rap! They growled. But Tony wasn't there. He was at his Grandma's house helping to make Christmas puddings. So the bears went away.

On Wednesday the bears were back once more. The middle-sized bear brought her two tumbling bear cubs with her. The big bear knocked on the front door. *Knock-knock-knock!* He knocked on the back door. *Clonk-clonk-clonk!* The cubs climbed up on the window-sills and looked through the windows. And they growled. But Tony wasn't there. He was at his Grandma's house helping to make Christmas biscuits.

On Thursday, along came the bears again. The tiger came, too.

The bears knocked on the front door. *Thump! Thump! Thump!* They knocked on the back door. *Bump! Bump! Bump!* The cubs looked through the windows. They all growled. Tiger, too! He prowled round the house growling and growling. Where was Tony? At his Grandma's house helping to make Christmas drinks.

Then it was Friday. Back they came: the bears and the tiger *and* the giraffe. She looked down the chimney while the bears hammered on the doors, the cubs looked in the windows and the tiger prowled round the house growling louder than the bears. Tony wasn't there. He was at his Grandma's house helping to make Christmas sweets.

The next day was Saturday. It was Christmas Eve. The animals went to Tony's house again. The monkeys came with them, running up the path ahead of everyone. They tried to look under the door and through the keyhole. They swung on the door bell and climbed on the door frame. "Oh, do behave!" said the middle-sized bear as the door opened with a swish.

"Come in!" said Tony. "I'm glad to see you."

In went the animals, into Tony's house. Most of the giraffe had to stay outside, but her head fitted through a window so she could be at Tony's party with the others. It was a Christmas party for his friends. His Grandma had helped him to get it ready.

They played party games, wore party hats and ate up the party food and drinks. They had honey cakes and Christmas honey pudding, striped tiger toffees and long drinks of jungle juice. And there were piles of monkey-nut biscuits.

Too soon it was time for the animals to go back to the zoo. "Happy Christmas!" they said. "Thank you for a lovely time, Tony!"

"Happy Christmas!" said Tony. "Thank you for coming to my party. I hope I see you again soon."

And maybe Tony did.

JOLLY SMILING COOK

This cook never gets tired or cross or cranky. He is made from a tin. Crumple a paper table napkin for his cap. Paste it to the top of a tin. Tidy up the edges with a long narrow strip of white paper pasted on firmly. It's the band about the cook's cap.

His round eyes and turned-up mouth are cut from paper and glued into place. If he looks like a chap who'd wear a moustache or beard then fix those for him.

When he's finished he can become a present—maybe for someone who likes to have barbecues.

If you like to cook, wear a cap made from a white paper-bag, big enough to fit your head. Wear an apron, too, just like a proper chef. A tea-towel tied about your middle will do. And before you make anything be sure that it's all right with the real cook at your place. It's very easy to be burned, so only make Tiger Toffee when there is a bigger person to help by handling the hot liquids. The best chefs always have helpers.

GOODIES TO MAKE

Tiger Toffee

Put into a big saucepan *1 cup of sugar* with *½ cup of water*. Stir and stir without stopping until the mixture boils and all the sugar dissolves. This is important if you want good toffee. Stop stirring now. Let the mixture cook on for about nine minutes, just gently bubbling. Take it off the stove.

Wait until the bubbles disappear from the toffee before pouring it into a greased tin, or into little paper pattycake cups.

Sprinkle the toffee with coconut, or crushed nuts, or hundreds and thousands. The toffee can be coloured with red, or yellow, or green food colouring.

Christmas Honey Cake for Bears and People

Melt *3 tablespoons of white vegetable shortening* with *1 tablespoon of sugar* and *1 tablespoon of honey*.

Pour this mixture over *1 cup of cornflakes, 1 cup of coconut* and some *crushed nuts* and *chopped raisins*.

Mix it all together.

Don't eat it yet, but spoon it into coloured paper cake cups. Top each little honey cake with a cherry.

Hide them in the refrigerator overnight, then eat with bears and people.

Christmas Pudding

Into a bowl put

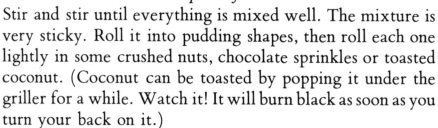
½ *tin of condensed milk*
½ *packet of plain crushed biscuits*
½ *cup of coconut*
½ *cup of cherries and chopped dates and dried fruits*
1 *tablespoon of cocoa*

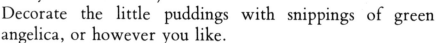

Stir and stir until everything is mixed well. The mixture is very sticky. Roll it into pudding shapes, then roll each one lightly in some crushed nuts, chocolate sprinkles or toasted coconut. (Coconut can be toasted by popping it under the griller for a while. Watch it! It will burn black as soon as you turn your back on it.)

Decorate the little puddings with snippings of green angelica, or however you like.

Monkey-nut Biscuits

Ask someone to make you some vanilla icing. You may like to turn some of it into chocolate by adding some cocoa. Spread the icing over plain oval or round biscuits. Give each one a monkey face by using crushed nuts, chocolate shavings, cherries and peel.

Pale-face Biscuits

Who wants to eat sweet things all the time? Try these. Cover plain round biscuits with cottage or cream cheese, then add faces by using rings of gherkins, slivers of pineapple, rings of pickled onions and other savoury ingredients.

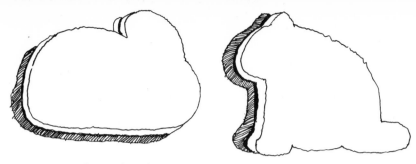

Animal Sandwiches

Make sandwiches from your favourite fillings using one slice of brown bread and one slice of white bread. Cut them into animal shapes with scone or biscuit-cutters. Stand the animals in a paddock of finely shredded lettuce grass, celery-stick trees and a hedge of radish roses.

Jungle Juice

Do you like orange juice? Pineapple juice? Mix them together and you've made jungle juice. Float some banana rings on the top.

Or mash a banana until it is very soft. Stir it into milk with a blob of ice-cream to make a different jungle drink. A well-beaten egg can be plopped in, too, or chocolate powder and vanilla. Or mix the egg, chocolate, vanilla and icecream with the milk, give it a whirl with the beater and it's Tiger Milk!

Marshmallow Snowmen

Stick two round marshmallows together with a little white icing. Use more of the icing to stick on currant eyes and buttons down the snowman's front. He can have a cherry mouth if you like, and a ribbon round his neck. Don't eat the ribbon!

Log Cake

Buy a Swiss roll. Cover it in rich chocolate icing, then mark it with a fork to look like a log. Now you have a *bouche de Noel*, a French Christmas cake.

DECISION

"Pudding and pie!" said Jane,
"Oh my! Pudding and pie!"

"Which would you rather?"
Asked her father. "Pudding or pie?"

"Both!" said Jane,
Quite loud and plain.
"Both pudding and pie . . . *please!*"

SKY HIGH PIE

One Monday, Sir Henry Grey said to Dorothy, his cook, "Make me a pie that is bigger than any that ever was." So she found twelve husky lads on the nearby farms to help her make the greatest pie that was ever baked.

They took butter and milk, salt, pepper and flour and made a dough, high up like a tower. Their rolling pin was a sawn-off tree and it took all twelve to push it free over the lumps in the pastry crust which fitted then into a tin newly-built and one hundred metres round.

And into that crust went—

    two bags of carrots
    four wild ducks,
    six young woodcocks
    four fat geese,
    two plump rabbits
    with impeccable habits,
    ten Best York hams
    sixty brown pigeons,
    lamb chops without number,
    a handful of thyme and
    crisply fried bacon rind.

Last of all, slowly poured, the richest of gravy was mixed through and through using an oar from the navy.

Meantime, an oven was built out in the yard but to get the pie there was almost too hard. Through the door it would not fit, so down came a wall, and they trundled it out on wheels, fixed by a cable to the mixing table.

They baked it for hours, then four hours more, and the smell of it brought dogs galore. Cats came by too, and so did people, to peep at the crust rising high like a steeple.

When at last it was done Henry roared with glee, "Bring a wagon! We'll take it to His Majesty!"

But the pie was too large to fit any cart, so Sir Henry said, "Fetch a ladder. I'll cut it in half."

A ladder was fetched. He climbed it, poor wretch, with his sword buckled to his side. He hacked at the crust: gravy came in a rush and Sir Henry, poor Henry, fell in! He'd have drowned then and there; not one stroke could he swim — had they not fished him out with the tree rolling-pin.

Sir Henry, poor Henry had swallowed much pie: if he rode now to London he surely would die, so he groaned, "A second-hand pie is not fit for a king. You eat it up and may it bring you a happy Christmas and a prosperous New Year."

So folk grouped about and ate up the pie, with crumbs left over for dogs called Rover and any others that came nosing by, plus everyone's cat, so that was that until another day, when Sir Henry Grey said to Dorothy, his cook, "Make me . . ."

—Well, what did Sir Henry want made? You decide. If it was another pie, start the story all over again. If it was something else, make up a new story about Sir Henry.

ST THOMAS' DAY IS PAST AND GONE

Once there was a time when Christmas pies were always filled with meat, poultry, or game. They were treats to look forward to. Bobby certainly looked forward to his Christmas pie!

St Thomas' Day is past and gone,
And Christmas almost come,
Maidens arise,
And make your pies,
And save poor Bobby some.

Four days before Christmas, on St Thomas' Day, village women set out a-Thomassing, visiting neighbours to collect enough flour for their Christmas baking. Bobby and other boys must have done a lot of loitering about the kitchens then. If Bobby lived in the North of England, and if he wanted a happy year he would beg at least one pie each day from the cook-girl during the twelve days of Christmas.

*"As many mince pies as you taste at Christmas,
so many happy months will you have," people said.*

Bobby would need to cadge and eat twelve pies for his happy year!

LITTLE JACK HORNER

Little Jack Horner sat in a corner,
Eating a Christmas pie;
He put in his thumb and pulled out a plum
And said, "What a good boy am I!"

JACK HORNER'S PLUM

Nowadays, Christmas pies are mostly made from fruits.
They are rich and spicy, oozing with currants and raisins and
sultanas, tangy lemon and orange peel and apples. The plum
in Jack Horner's pie was a prune.

THE PLUM GAME

There is a game named after Jack Horner's pie. This is one
way to play it. The 'pie' is a big box, or a carton. Hide inside
it as many 'plums' as there are players. Each plum is a tiny
gift of some kind with an enormously long string tied to it.
The string wanders about the playing area. If it goes under a
table then the player must follow it, winding up his string as
he goes. If it goes over a chair so does the player. If it twists
and twines about another player's string it must be untangled
before he can go on. The string can travel anywhere, all over
the house maybe, but it finally ends at the 'pie' box. The
player then pulls out his 'plum' present. It can be something
very silly, something to eat, anything you choose. How
about a bonbon? You could make some.

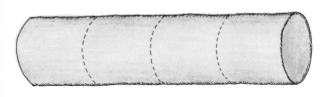

BONBONS TO MAKE

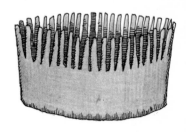

The bonbon cases can be made from a lunch-wrap tube. Cut it into four pieces.

Use crêpe paper to cover each cardboard piece of tubing, but first, you'll need surprises to go inside each bonbon.

Usually there is a party hat. Cut some crêpe paper to head-size and fasten it with staples, sticky-tape or glue. Decorate it, or cut the hat into a crown.

Often there is a joke or a riddle inside a bonbon. Write some on scraps of paper. Here are some tongue-twisters you could use as well:

> The sixth sheik's sixth sheep's sick.
> Flo fried fresh fish.
> Grey geese grazing on green grass.
> The sun shines on shop signs.

Tiny gifts can go into the bonbon tube if you have any. (Remember the lucky wishbones.) Roll the tube in bright crêpe paper. Tie off the ends firmly, leaving enough paper free to shred, and paste on a decoration.

GAMES TO PLAY

It doesn't have to be Christmas and you don't need to have a party to play these games. Play them at any time with your friends. Grown-ups can join in and so can very small children.

Hot Cockles

Hot Cockles, however, is in fact an old Christmas game. One player lies down in the middle of the floor. He is blindfolded. The rest of the players walk about him. Every so often some one touches his shoulder, or knee, or toe and calls out in a very silly voice, "Hot Cockles!" If the teasing player can be named correctly by the blindfolded person, then the teaser must take his turn to do the guessing. Down on the floor with him. On with the blindfold and on with the game.

Snapdragon

This is another old game. Raisins are put into a shallow dish, some brandy poured over, then set alight. Snatch a raisin before the fiery dragon can burn your fingers! To be safer still, wait until the fire goes out!

Apple Dangle

Have you tried to eat an apple dangling from a string? You must not touch it with your hands. Keep them behind your back. Have a go!

Floating Apples

Have you tried to bite into an apple that's floating in a bowl of water? Don't touch it with any part of your body except your face. This is a wet game, very wet!

Peanut Hunt

The oldest to the youngest can join a peanut hunt. It's best played out of doors. The peanuts are hidden about the garden, and then the hunt is on. The person to find the most peanuts is the winner, but everyone gets a prize. Sit down and eat every peanut you've found.

Colour Spy

Here's a game to play on a long car trip, or when time must be filled in—perhaps while waiting for a plane to come in, or sitting in a dentist's waiting room. Each player must try to guess a secret. The only clue given is a colour. It can be any colour, but the secret thing must be in the room, the car, or wherever you are. Often it's easy to guess, sometimes it's very hard.

Clothes Race

Put lots of odd pieces of clothes into two boxes. It doesn't matter about the shapes or sizes or what kind of clothes are collected. Two people must *walk*—no running now—up to the boxes, starting at a given signal. They put on the clothes as fast as they can. Each button must be fastened. Zips closed. Ribbons and strings tied. Hooks and press-studs fixed. Then, *without running,* first one back to the starting point is the winner.

Another way to play the clothes game is with music. There is a box of clothes to be shared by the ones who want to play. The music begins. Whoever can put on the most clothes before it stops is the winner. There isn't any rule about doing up zips and buttons this time—just get going as fast as you can.

SING, SING

Sing, sing,
> What shall I sing?
The cat's run away
> With the pudding string!

Do, Do,
> What shall I do?
The cat's run away
> With the pudding too!

The old way to cook a Christmas pudding was to roll it in a cloth and tie it with string, then boil the pudding for hours and hours. In some families good puddings may still be made like that. And in some families, when the pudding is being mixed everyone comes to stir it and to make a wish. Grandpa comes, Grandma comes and someone holds the baby's hand to help him stir. Everyone keeps their Christmas wish as a secret. If it is told a wish will *never* come true.

106

CHRISTMAS PUDDING

Into the pudding put the plums,
Stir about, stir about, stir about all.

Next the good white flour comes,
Stir about, stir about, stir about all.

Sugar and peel and eggs and spice,
Stir about, stir about, stir about all.

This is the way our pudding's done,
Stir about, stir about, stir about all.

Try it yourself and have some fun,
Stir about, stir about, stir about all.

Find actions to go with the rhyme

Into many Christmas puddings go small silver coins, or tiny silver trinkets—perhaps a little horseshoe, a wishbone, a ring, a bell, a button. It's good luck if you find one in your slice of pudding. And whoever finds the bachelor button won't be married before the next Christmas pudding is made.

LITTLE PLUM DUFF

Mr Duffy drove a delivery truck for one of the city stores. Christmas was a busy time for him. So many parcels had to be delivered to people's houses. Big ones, fat ones, heavy ones, lumpy ones!

While he was out one morning, fine misty rain began to fall. Swish-swish went his windscreen wipers as he drove along. "Drat it!" grumbled Mr Duffy as the rain became heavier. "I've forgotten my raincoat."

So, when he came to the next house, he made a fast dash for its door with a parcel under his arm. The truck's cabin door swung open.

A little stray cat looked into the cabin. It was dry inside. In jumped the cat. He shook his wet paws, he shook the raindrops from his fur and then settled down under the dashboard. *Prrrr*, said the cat.

Mr Duffy raced back to his truck, pulled the door shut and drove on to make his next delivery. He didn't see the cat. In fact, he was too busy to notice the cat all through the morning. The cat did not make a sound.

By lunchtime Mr Duffy was back in the city. He stopped for some traffic lights, waiting in a line of cars and other trucks.

"Meouw!" said the cat.

108

Mr Duffy looked to the footpath, expecting to see a cat. But there were only people walking along. No cat! People were crossing the street, too. No cat was with them. He looked at the car waiting beside him. Only a man was in it. No cat!

"Funny, I thought I heard a cat," said Mr Duffy.

The traffic lights turned green then. Brrrummm! Mr Duffy was on his way again.

"Meouw!" said the cat in a thin high voice, too high and thin to be heard over the engine's sound. "Meww!" said the cat and jumped up on the seat beside Mr Duffy. It rubbed its head against his arm.

"Lumme!" exploded Mr Duffy. "The cat's in my truck!"

"Mewwwwww!" answered the cat.

It was no use Mr Duffy saying, "Get, Cat! Scat!" Not in town traffic. He didn't know where it had come from. He didn't know what to do with it. And it was such a skinny little cat. He took it back to the store where he ate his lunch. The cat watched Mr Duffy bite into a sandwich. "Meouw!" it pleaded.

Mr Duffy took another bite.

"Meouwww!" cried the cat, staring at the sandwich.

"Cats don't eat cheese," said Mr Duffy, tossing it some cheese from his bread. But that cat did eat cheese, all the cheese in Mr Duffy's lunch. And Mr Duffy ate bread-and-butter.

Mr Duffy drank strong black tea. The cat drank the milk he usually poured into it. Then it curled up on some wrapping paper and went to sleep.

All the week the cat stayed in the storeroom. Mr Duffy brought it meat and milk from home each day, right up to Christmas Eve. On Christmas Eve, just before he left the store, Mr Duffy set out a pile of meat and a big bowl of milk, enough food to last the cat for at least three days, three holidays.

"That will keep you going until I come back after the Christmas break," he told the skinny little cat. Then Mr Duffy set off for the bus stop "Would that milk stay fresh?" he asked himself. No, it would not, not for three days! And the meat wouldn't either. Maybe the skinny little cat would eat all the meat at once and then be hungry before the next evening. "How can I eat my Christmas dinner if that cat is hungry?" thought Mr Duffy. He turned about and went back to the store.

He picked up the skinny little cat, looking about for something to carry it in. There were plenty of paper bags and large sheets of paper. Nothing else! He put the cat into a big roomy bag, and with its head poking out from the top they went to the bus stop.

"Mewwww!" howled the skinny little cat.

"Now, look here, Mate, you can't take that cat on the bus," said the conductor. "No cats allowed on this bus."

"But it's Christmas, can't . . ." mumbled Mr Duffy.

"No cats on the bus!" said the driver this time. "Sorry, Mate!"

"No cats in this taxi," said a taxi driver when Mr Duffy hailed his cab.

I CAN FIT IN A TINY PAPER BAG!

So Mr Duffy, with the skinny cat in a paper bag, walked home.

It was late when he went through his door. His dinner was spoiled. His wife didn't scold. She was glad to see him home and gave him a kiss. Mr Duffy's little girl kissed him too, and his little boy hugged and hugged him.

"I couldn't leave this skinny little chap in the store over Christmas," Mr Duffy told his wife sheepishly.

"We'll keep him," she said. "He's no one's cat."

"He's our Christmas cat!" corrected the children.

Within weeks the skinny little Christmas cat had grown into a round, fat, contented Christmas cat with glossy dark fur and bright eyes. Mr Duffy called him his little Plum Duff, the old name for a Christmas pudding. And Plum Duff is still with the family to this very day.

FRUITY PERCY

This rhyme is about a pudding, not the Duffy's Christmas cat.

Fruity Percy Plum Duff,
Pop him in a pot.
Slice him up,
Serve him up,
Eat him while he's hot.

A PUDDING TO MAKE

Here's a pudding you can make. It is not cooked. It is eaten cold.

Chop up coarsely all these things . . .

1½ cup of prunes
1 cup of dates
1 cup of dried apricots
1 cup of walnuts

Mix the fruit and nuts together, then put them aside while you mix together

¼ cup of sugar
¼ cup of concentrated orange juice

When the sugar has dissolved, pour the orange juice over the fruits and mix it in well. Roll it into a plump pudding ball and then in chocolate shavings or chopped nuts. Put the pudding into the refrigerator to firm. It is very rich, so serve only small portions. And as it's a sticky cooking job, you may lick your fingers—but only when you've finished.

THE RED CAP

One day long ago, a blacksmith lost his way through a wood thick with trees. Not only was he lost, but it was almost dark. The man knew that he had been foolish to leave the road.

Earlier in the afternoon he had returned a newly-shod horse to its owner. It was such a long trudge back to his own village that he decided upon the short cut through the trees. Now he was lost. "I'll go back to the road," he thought; but when he turned to retrace his steps he found the path was no longer behind him! Strange to say, the trees closed into a thick hedge. His way back was blocked. "I must be dreaming," muttered the blacksmith, and before he had time to pinch himself to discover if he were dreaming, he heard children's voices. Children shrieking with laughter! Children shouting from joy! "Where there's children there will be men and women," decided the blacksmith. "Some one will be able to direct me back to the road."

And so he stepped out along the twisting track, following the sounds. He came to a clearing, and sure enough, small figures were darting across it. However, the blacksmith did not go on . . . not yet. There was something odd about the look of the children and the sounds of their shrill voices. "Not one of my children runs about so wildly, or sounds like that," thought the blacksmith. He had seven of them at home.

He stepped behind a tree and peered through the eerie, green forest light. "Heaven save me!" he gasped. "They are dwarfs! No! I don't believe it! I must be dreaming!"

And just then, he saw a little red cap dangling from a branch near his head. The cap was so small it could only have fitted a dwarf, or the blacksmith's babe at home. "Heaven help me!" he whispered. "Those little beasties will want to bewitch me! What am I to do?"

What he did was to stare out at the dwarfs again. And a great time they were having! They danced and chased and jumped and wrestled. They threw their red caps in the air, or kicked them like footballs. And behind the rollicking dwarfs, others sat at the remains of a feast. The table was a mess. Dishes were broken, goblets overturned, food and wine were spilt. One dwarf snored drunkenly with his head in a bowl. Others were throwing cakes and sausages and pies at each other, and the rest were stuffing their mouths with food, then spitting it out in some sort of a competition.

That was too much for the blacksmith! He was so poor he rarely had two pennies to rub together. His children were thin and half-fed. The waste of food appalled him. "Stop that at once, you dirty little beasties!" he shouted at the dwarfs.

There was silence, a *long* silence! The dwarfs gawked at the angry blacksmith, then, growling and grumbling they dived about the clearing to snatch up their red caps. The caps were dragged on to their heads, down over their ears and then ... *whssst!* the dwarfs and their feast were gone. They had disappeared completely.

AREN'T THEY BEING HORRIBLE?

No: one little fellow remained. He was jumping about the tree near the blacksmith, trying to reach the little red cap that dangled there. He jumped and he sobbed and he looked beseechingly at the blacksmith. "Aaah! you can't leave without your cap, is that it?" asked the blacksmith, handing the cap down to the dwarf.

The cap was snatched without a word of thanks. The dwarf dragged it down on his head and over his ears. *Whsst!* And he, too, disappeared.

The next instant, strange to say, the blacksmith found himself outside his own door. He was a very puzzled man. Had he been dreaming? Yes, his wife agreed that he had been dreaming when she heard his story. "No one will believe such a tale," he decided. So he kept his adventure to himself.

That night, before going to his bed, the blacksmith went into his workship to leave his tools ready for the next morning's work.

Next morning, he was astonished to find the forge fire was alight and his tools scattered about the floor as if someone had been disturbed whilst at work. Stranger still, his work was done—and finer craftmanship the Smithy had never seen. There were horseshoes fit for the steeds of a prince, and an iron gate strong enough to guard a palace. Splendid work! Who had done it? The blacksmith hadn't heard the clang of iron, or the tap of a single hammer during the night. Nor did he hear anything the following nights, but each morning his work was done, perfectly done. Who was doing it?

"We'll stay awake tonight and discover our friend," he told his wife. And at midnight, there they stood, yawning

116

and nodding behind the draught curtain of rough bagging which hung in the workshop.

Dong! Dong! The village clock began to strike twelve. *Whsst!* out of nowhere appeared a dwarf, pulling a little red cap from his head. Carefully he stowed the cap in the pocket of his tattered coat, stomped across the workshop floor and went to work. *Clang-clang-tap-tap!* He hammered red-hot iron into shape. *Clang-clang-tap-tap!* He worked until dawn. Then he dragged the cap over his head, down over his ears and *whssst!* he was gone.

"It was the dwarf I helped in the forest!" the blacksmith told his wife.

Night after night, the dwarf helped the Smithy with his work until he was famous all over the countryside for his speed and craftmanship. Soon his children were rosy-cheeked and fat, and wore warm jackets and woollen stockings.

"I'll make Little Red Cap a new suit of clothes, too," said the blacksmith's wife. "His own clothes are no better than rags. I'll have new ones for him by Christmas."

So she cut and stitched a little brown suit from the best woollen cloth. It was belted with the finest copper buckle the blacksmith had ever made. Their eldest daughter stitched a little shirt from cream silk. And the next daughter knitted two long stockings from the finest brown wool. The eldest son cut and sewed a pair of shoes from fine red leather. The youngest son found a curling white feather for the dwarf to wear in his red cap.

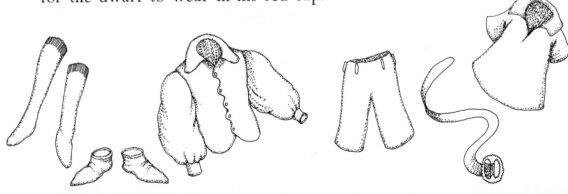

On Christmas Eve, the blacksmith and his family crowded behind the draught curtain of bagging. The pile of clothes stood on the bench near the Smithy's forge.

Dong! Dong! The village clock struck the hour of twelve. *Whssst!* out of nowhere appeared the dwarf, pulling the little red cap from his head. He stomped to the bench and saw the pile of clothes. He whooped. He tore off his tattered coat and breeches. He put on the shirt. He put on the brown suit made from the best woollen cloth. He put on the stockings. He pushed the little curling feather into his cap. Then he pranced and preened up and down the workship. Then, with a wide grin, he turned to the curtain of bagging and swept down in a deep and gracious bow.

Next thing, the red cap was on his head, pulled down over his ears and *whsssst!* he was gone.

The blacksmith and his family never saw the little dwarf again, but they never forgot his kindness, and they told his story each year at Christmas time.

NASTY LITTLE BEASTIES

Trolls, sly like ghost-ies, sit-ting up-on post - ies,

Eat-ing but-tered toast-ies, Gob-bling down the most - ies.

Smeared with greas-ies, Run-ning down their cheek - sies,

Drip-ping off their knees-ies, Nas-ty lit-tle beast - ies!

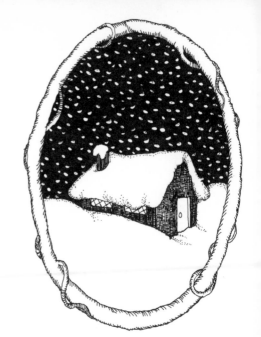

SNOWFLAKES FALLING
Bright snow
iced snow
cold snow
light snow
flaked and white delight snow
fall soft on Christmas night.

SNOWFLAKES TO MAKE

Here's a quick way to make snowflakes to decorate a window or a glass door.

You'll need pairs of paper-lace doilies, long threads of dark cotton and some glue.

Brush some glue over one doily. Lay a thread across it, letting a long end hang freely. Press the second doily on top. Let the snowflake dry, then hang it up. Small doilies make the best snowflakes. Varied sizes and patterns look their best if hung at different lengths. You may like to use silver or gold doilies. Or you can colour the white ones with chalks, paints or crayons.

Foil Snowflakes

A quicker way to make snowflakes is to cut squares of kitchen foil. Fold each square into yet another square, and then into a triangle. Snip out a snowflake pattern. Unfold. Now you have a Christmas tree ornament.

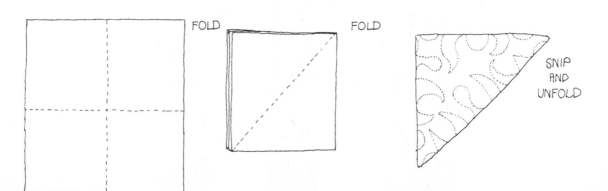

FOLD   FOLD   SNIP AND UNFOLD

Carved Snowflakes

If you like carving and are good at it, go to work with thin balsa wood and whittle a handful of snowflakes. Dye them with vegetable colouring, paint them or leave them the natural wood colour.

Tissue Snowflakes

This snowflake is harder to make.
Collect together scissors, clear glue, coloured tissue-papers, a brush and some clear kitchen plastic—the clinging kind.

Cut squares from the tissue papers and the plastic. Fold the tissue inside the plastic and it will be easier to cut. It doesn't matter if your edges aren't trim and even.

Now fold the squares into smaller squares and then into triangles. Snip out a snowflake pattern. Unfold. Glue one tissue snowflake to a plastic snowflake. When it is dry, glue a second tissue snowflake in a *different* colour over the first tissue. Let it dry. Trim the edges of the plastic.

The snowflake is ready to be pressed on to a window. First, make sure that the plastic and the window glass are clean; then the snowflakes will cling without trouble. If the edges curl, push them back into place with a damp cloth.

By using contrasting colours, your snowflake will be delicately translucent as the light shines through it.

PAPER AND CARDS TO MAKE

Most presents are hidden under crackly crisp paper. You can make your own paper to wrap your gifts. Scrap papers, tissue-paper and newspapers can be decorated. So can white and brown papers. Experiment first, then find the way you like working best.

Finger Paint

If you need finger paint, here are two ways to make it. Just colour some liquid starch with powder paint or some food colouring, the kind that is used to make coloured icings for cakes.

For larger amounts of finger paint use this recipe:
Slowly blend ½ *cup of cornflour* with *1 cup of cold water.*
Put in a little cooking salt.
Bring the mixture slowly to the boil. STIR ALL THE TIME, otherwise your paint will be lumpy and gluggy. Let it cool.
Slowly add powder paint or food colouring.

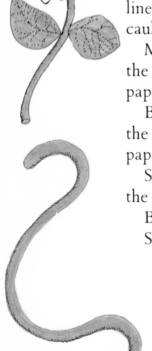

To keep the finger paint as smooth as custard, add a few drops of liquid soap, or detergent. Keep it in airtight containers.

You can finger-paint in squiggles, swirls, wiggles, and lines of all kinds. You can print with sprigs of broccoli and cauliflower, daisies and gum nuts.

Make curved lines by pulling wool soaked in paint across the paper. Soak string in finger paint and pull it over damp paper for a lovely blotched look.

Build patterns with dots and spots made by printing with the end of a straw, or blow paint from the straw over the paper.

Squish on a design with half a lemon or an orange. Let the slice of fruit dry overnight for a different effect.

Blob on paint with the end of a cotton reel.

Sweep a brush full of paint over the paper. Sweep

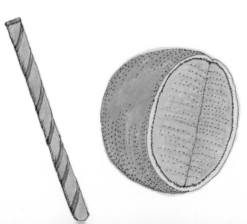

another brush in the opposite way. Use two colours, three colours, four colours.

Spatter designs through a strainer. Spatter over leaves or flowers, grasses or seeds, or paper shapes laid on the wrapping paper.

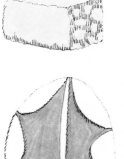

Draw with a felt pen on damp paper. Don't wet the paper too much, just dampen it, and then draw gently, otherwise the paper may tear.

Dab a pattern with a sponge dipped into paint.

Scratch or scrawl a design over layers of crayoned colours.

Make a holly print with a potato cut. Find a small potato and cut it in half. The cleaner the cut, the better. On one half cut a narrow strip from the top to the bottom. If one side of this can be cut on a slant the strip will lift out easily. Now cut three curved slices from each side to make the leaf shape. Blot off juices. Use green tempera paint on tissue paper or plain white paper to stamp out a pattern of holly leaves. The rubber tip of a pencil dipped into red paint will give fat rounded holly berries.

And now, if you like the idea, make cards to match the papers. Most of the painting methods we've talked about can be used.

Make some cards very small. Make some very, very huge. What shape? A circle? A house? An animal? A tree? A spaceship? A flower? A fat man? A laughing face?

Christmas cards can be cut into Christmas shapes, too. Try a bell, or a bonbon, a holly leaf, a Christmas wreath, a cake, tree decorations or even a Nisse.

You can make a card from a picture you've painted. Fold it into wide pleats, the way you would make a fan. The card will stand alone then. This card looks very special if it's painted on both sides. Use heavy paper to do that, then the paint won't show through on the other side. Other cards can be made by decorating the paper with collage patterns made from torn papers, or scraps of old Christmas cards.

Yet another way is to cut out squares or circles of cardboard. Paste a picture on it, or a paper cut-out silhouette. Or make decorations from paper flowers, shreds of paper, tinsel, feathers, laces or paper doilies. Or sew a picture from coloured wools and cottons. Perhaps you could combine the ideas.

Sprinkle cards with sequins or glitter. Brush first with paste.

Make cones from paper. Some can become little Christmas trees, others can be Santa Claus, or clowns. Santa, of course, wears a red cap. Paint it on. Trim the cap with white paper, cotton wool, or pieces of lace doily. Use the same trim for his beard.

Draw shapes or faces or a pattern on a coloured card. Brush with glue, then follow the pencilled lines with white string, both thick and thin.

Print lots of cards from your own designs with your own printing blocks. Make the pattern for each block by cutting a simple shape from plastic foam. Just an outline is often enough. Glue the foam to a block; a nailbrush will do. Brush paint lightly on the design then press it down on the paper you want to print. Have a trial run before going to work. The same block can be used to make matching papers for the cards.

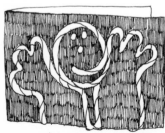

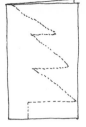

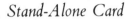

Stand-Alone Card

You will need firm wrapping paper, or painted paper, or heavy typing paper, or newsprint. Cut three pieces the same size. Fold each one in half and crease firmly down the middle. On each piece draw the shape of *half* a tree, working outwards from the fold. Cut along the shape. Do not unfold the papers. Place two shapes together with the folded sides meeting. Join them with sticky tape. Now fold one paper back against its mate, down the line of sticky tape. Place the third shape beside it, making sure that the creased sides meet each other. Stick them together with tape. Trim the bottom edges evenly so the tree will stand. Unfold, and the tree stands alone. Decorate the six sides with small toys, or decorations.

Here's an idea for a lacy snowflake card. Make your own from white or silver or gold lace doilies. Cut some coloured papers into circles just a little smaller than the doilies you plan to use. Place one coloured paper inside each doily then fold both papers in half at the same time. Sew or staple them together, or use a bright ribbon bow.

Make an angel card by using a lace doily for wings. First, draw the outline of an angel on a card or paper. Keep it very simple. Cut the doily into wings and paste them in place. Paste on a robe. It can be made by pleating white paper or cutting corrugated or textured papers into a robe—or else use material. Last of all, give the angel a halo, a circlet of gold twine, ribbon, or string. Or you can paint the halo.

A RING OF ANGELS TO MAKE

An angel ring is meant to be hung high overhead: then the angels look as if they are flying.

Start by making the ring from a circle of wire. If you can't find any wire, use a narrow strip of firm cardboard and fasten it into a circle. The angels can be made from cardboard too, or else use kitchen foil. Cut out as many angels as you've decided to fix to the ring. Keep each shape very simple. Decorate the angels if you want to do that. Fasten the angels to the ring by stapling or glueing, or with a few stitches of thread. Space each one an equal distance from its neighbour. You could add some sprigs of greenery, baubles or other decorations.

Last of all tie on three strings to the ring, spacing them at equal distances from each other. Now tie the string-ends together so that the angel ring will be evenly balanced when it is hung. It would make a present for someone you especially like.

A Kissing Ring

A kissing ring is made the same way by using mistletoe and apples. Anyone caught standing under the ring of mistletoe must pay a forfeit of a kiss.

126

THE SECRET

It was holiday time for Andrew. Christmas holidays! He wouldn't be going to school again for weeks and weeks.

Tucked inside his school bag were secret surprises. "Presents for everyone," he told Suzie in a mysterious whisper. "Christmas presents! I made them at school."

Suzie badly wanted to know what the surprises were. She wanted to know there and then. "I want to see them, Andrew," she said. "Please, Andrew-Andrew-Andrew, pleease!"

"No!" Andrew was being very firm. "No, Suzie! If you look the presents won't be surprises any more."

"Then just tell me what is inside the parcels," she begged.

"No! If I tell you they won't be secrets."

"Then can't I just feel them and guess what's inside?" asked Suzie.

"No, no, *no*!" said Andrew, and he ran away laughing.

"Can't I have a secret too?" Suzie called after him. Then she thought, "I wish I had a secret. If I were as big as Andrew and went to school, I could have a secret."

Andrew really hoped that Suzie would forget about the presents, and he put them away in a hiding-place, a secret place in his cupboard.

Suzie didn't forget. She went to Mummy. "I wish I had a secret like Andrew's."

"But you do! You have a secret already," Mummy told her.

"I can't think of any," Suzie said. "I don't think I have one, not even a very little one."

WISH I HAD A SECRET TOO!

"Oh, yes, you do!" her mother told her. "Come close. I'll remind you." She bent over Suzie. Suzie stretched up to hear Mummy's whisper. *Ssss. Sssssss. Sssssss!* The whisper tickled Suzie's ear. She curled up her shoulder and giggled, then she hugged Mummy. "Yes, I do have a secret surprise."

Andrew heard that Suzie had a surprise. And he wanted to know what it was.

"It's a Christmas present for all the family and it's a secret," Suzie told him.

"*All* the family! Gosh, is it something to eat?"

"No, nothing to eat."

"Is it something big?"

"No."

"Then it must be little?"

"No! It's not big and not little. I can't even wrap it up."

"*Not* wrap it up!" Andrew shouted with surprise. "It must be a very funny thing if it can't be wrapped up."

"It's not funny! It's lovely!" And Suzie hugged herself with joy as she thought of her surprise.

"Does it smell, then?" asked Andrew.

"No, of course it doesn't smell. Don't be silly!" chuckled Suzie. "You can't smell it. You can't even see it. And you can't feel it. And I'm not going to tell you what it is." And Suzie didn't tell, although Andrew kept pestering her about her surprise right up to Christmas Eve.

On Christmas morning Andrew put his surprise parcels under the tree. They were wrapped in paper he had finger-painted himself. Andrew had made his cards, too. Suzie's was shaped like a gingerbread man.

"Open up the presents," Andrew said.

128

"What's this? What's this?" asked Dad. "I do believe it's an owl for me." And it was. The fattest, biggest pine-cone owl.

"I made his eyes and his beak and his two feet from felt," said Andrew. "They're stuck on with glue."

"And he's just the owl I need as a paper-weight," said Dad. "I like him."

"And I like my present, too," Mummy was saying. It was a pendant made from clay dough, a blue fish pendant hanging on a leather thong. "Thank you, Andrew!" she said and put it about her neck.

"Everyone look at my present!" Suzie was calling out. "Isn't it just the best thing?"

"It's a counting board," Andrew told her. "I made it so you can learn your colours as well as how to count."

"It's my counting Christmas tree!" decided Suzie. "Just look how Andrew has made it."

"So it is. Lucky Suzie!" said Mummy. "Now it's time for you to give everyone your present."

"But where is it?" Dad was looking about.

"It's a present you can't see," said Andrew. "And you can't feel it."

"It's not big and it's not little," said Suzie. "It can't be wrapped up."

"And it doesn't even have a smell," finished Andrew.

"Well fancy that!" said Dad. "I don't think Suzie has a present at all. It's a joke."

"Indeed it's not," laughed Mummy. "It's a very real present. Come along, Suzie."

Suzie stood by the Christmas tree. She smiled at everyone, and then she began to sing:

129

"I wish you a merry Christmas,
I wish you a merry Christmas,
I wish you a merry Christmas,
And a happy New Year."

Everyone clapped. Andrew and Dad had never heard her sing that song before. "It really was a surprise," said Dad. "Well done, Suzie!" But Suzie's surprise wasn't finished. She gave Dad a hug and a Christmas kiss. She gave Andrew a hug and a Christmas kiss. She gave Mummy lots of hugs because she had taught Suzie the Christmas song.

And for the rest of the day, Suzie was able to give her Christmas song to everyone who came to their house.

I WISH YOU A MERRY CHRISTMAS

SOME PRESENTS TO MAKE

Very often the best of presents can't be seen at all. They can be hugs or kisses or promises. A promise could be to help a grown-up with a job. To help tidy the garden maybe, or bring in the papers, or take out the empty milk bottles, or to carry shopping from the car. You are sure to think of other things you can do.

Often, too, the best of presents is one which has been especially found or made for someone.

It could be a shell or a stone to keep papers in place.

It could be a little bunch of dried grass tied with a bright ribbon.

It could be a pencil holder made from a tin. There are different ways to turn an ordinary tin into a special one.

First, soak the tin, then pull off the label. Dry it and re-cover it with one of your own paintings, or wallpaper, or torn scraps of different papers to make a collage pattern. Trim the edges, then glue ribbon, braid, lace or a paper frieze to the top of the tin.

Small tins can be used to hold odds and ends which are often lost in kitchen drawers. Big tins can be for storing pencils and pens. Very big tins make scrap tins or waste-paper bins.

Collect together some paper bags. Draw or paste a picture on each one. It can be a litter bag for someone's car. A bundle of litter bags can be kept in the glove-box.

Ordinary candles can become soldier-smart by winding coloured sticky tape about each one. Work sideways to get a spiralled jazzy look. Paper stars and other shapes can be pasted on candles, too.

Little lanterns can be made from tins. Fill the tins with water and leave in the refrigerator to become ice. Then it is easy to hammer a pattern of holes in the tins with a big nail. Make lots of holes. Don't forget the bottoms of the tins. And make holes near the rim, where a hanging string can be fastened. Let the ice melt. Dry the tin. Put a piece of candle in the bottom of each one. It may need to sit in a blob of plasticine. The little lanterns can be used for barbecues.

If you know someone who likes to wear pretty hairclips, glue a glittery button or a tiny ribbon bow to the rounded end of a hair grip.

Here's a way to make a rubbed-band keeper. Cut a tree shape from cardboard. Put a hole at the top and thread a loop of ribbon or string through it. Stretch some elastic bands across the tree to help decorate it. Add other decorations if you like. Little pine-cone drawings, perhaps, or fruit or flowers.

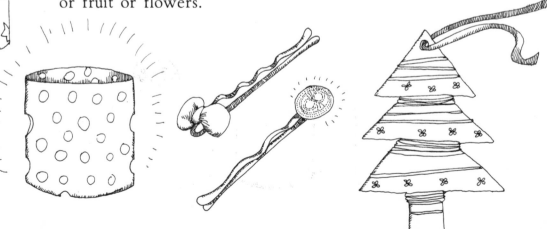

PINK SUGAR MOUSE

Only Simon knew what Kate wanted for Christmas. More than anything Kate wanted the tiny white plastic tea-set in the little blue box, on the toy shelf in the supermarket. "I love that tea-set," said Kate. She could hardly take her eyes off it.

"Don't you like this car better?" asked Simon. He didn't look at the tea-set. He'd just seen a red truck. "And what about this red truck? Brummm!"

"No, I like the tea-set," said Kate. "The car is nice, and so is the truck, but I like the little white cups and the little white saucers and the little white jug and the little white tea-pot and the little white basin for sugar. And look, Simon, every piece has the same little blue flowers on it!"

"But Katie, those cups are only about as big as . . . as big as my thumb nail!" Simon told her giving the tea-set a long look. "They're too small for anything. No one could drink from a cup as small as that!"

"I like the tea-set best, just the same," said Katie, "and I wish it were mine for Christmas."

And that's how Simon, and only Simon, knew what his little sister wanted for Christmas.

On Christmas Eve, Katie hung up her stocking soon after breakfast. Empty and small, it dangled from the shelf over the fireplace. Simon didn't want to hang his up until bedtime. And their big brother, Stephen, didn't know if he'd hang his up at all. He rushed off to play with his friends while Simon hurried away to the supermarket.

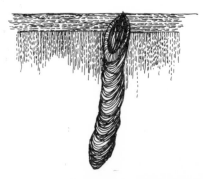

He spent a long time searching the toy shelves for the little blue box with the little white plastic tea-set inside it. "Some one must have bought it," he decided. He spent a long time then trying to decide what Katie would like almost as much as the tea-set. In the end he bought a little pink sugar mouse. And when he pushed it down into Katie's stocking it made a little fat bulge in the toe.

Stephen saw the bulge in Kate's stocking when he came home. He thought the toe had become tucked in by mistake. He put his hand into the stocking to straighten it. Out came the little sugar mouse.

Mmmm! It smelt . . . what did it smell of? Stephen sniffed the sugar mouse. Did it smell of honey, or was it almonds?

No! What was it? Without thinking of anything else, Stephen bit off one of the ears. It tasted of vanilla, yes, vanilla! He looked at the mouse. It looked silly and lopsided with just one ear. *Snap!* He bit off the second ear. Stephen laughed. It didn't look like a mouse at all now. He didn't know what it looked like. "I may as well eat it all," he thought. But the next mouthful of the pink sugar mouse almost choked him. "That mouse must have been a present for Kate from someone!" he thought. "I've eaten Katie's present!" he wailed.

Stephen went to his room and sat on the floor. The pink sugar mouse seemed to stick in his chest. "Katie won't miss the mouse," he told himself. "She didn't even know it was there."

He started to think about other things. But it was no use. His thoughts would go back to the pink sugar mouse. He remembered its pale-pink colour. He remembered that its eyes had been chocolate and its tail a long strip of licorice. Katie would have liked eating the mouse as much as he had.

Stephen put his hands into his pockets. He jingled the money that was there, then whistling to himself, he went off on his bike to the supermarket.

He walked up and down the aisle by the sweet shelves, looking for a pink sugar mouse. He couldn't find one.

"Maybe Kate would like a bag of chocolate frogs?" he thought. But they had been sold too. So had the chocolate cars and the chocolate bears. There wasn't even a bag of jelly babies left.

Stephen went to look amongst the toys for something to give Katie. Those shelves were almost empty too. Kate already had a bucket and spade. And a hairdressing set. She was too big for a squeaking-squeeze toy. But behind a bright yellow duck Stephen saw a little white box. Inside it was a tea-set. It was blue. Tiny white flowers decorated the cups. The cups were no bigger than a thimble. "Kate would like that," he decided; and so Stephen bought the tea-set.

"Look what I've found!" shouted Katie with delight the next morning when she opened the little white box. "It's just what I wanted. I wished for this!"

Stephen was very pleased to see Katie so happy. Simon was glad too, but he was puzzled. Later that morning Stephen and Simon drank pretend tea from the tiny cups and Simon was still wondering. How did a pink sugar mouse turn into a blue tea-set in a white box?

Then Katie said, "I thought I wanted a white tea-set more than anything. That's what I really wished for. But I like the blue one even better, yes, I do!"

And that was that! Simon stopped worrying and bothering straight away. No one really knows how Katie's wish came true—except you.

SUGAR AND SPICE AND LITTLE PINK MICE

Sugar and spice
And other things nice
Make sugar plums round
And little pink mice.

At one time sugar-plums were treats for children and the lucky grown-ups. Sugar was boiled and boiled, flavoured and delicately coloured. Then it was moulded into round or oval sugar plums, or little animals.

Make your own sugar-plums with marzipan which can be bought in packets.

Better still, try making your own. It's a sticky-icky-licky job!

Start with a mixing bowl, a roomy one. Put in some icing sugar.

Add a little pink vegetable colouring for pink animals. Use cocoa if you want brown animals.

Add some flavouring. That could be almond. Or it could be lemon, or cherry, or vanilla. Or you may like cinnamon, or ginger, or nutmeg. And there's orange and peppermint, too.

Now crush out any lumps in the icing sugar, then slowly add egg white, a little at a time. Mix it into the icing sugar. Keep on adding the egg white until the mixture is firm enough to make into shapes.

You can roll out the marzipan on a board which has been sprinkled with icing sugar to keep it from sticking. Or dust icing sugar over your hands to mould the animal shapes. If you use a cutter or knife, dip it into icing sugar occasionally.

137

Currants and cloves can be used for animals' eyes. Tiny sweets, cherries, angelica, bits of ginger or chocolate help to decorate the animals and sugar-plums. . Don't forget the animals' tails. Use licorice, or small pieces of string, ribbons or curled ends of pipe cleaners.

And after you've finished, clean up and wash up like the best cooks always do.

THUMB MOUSE

These animals are not sticky, but almost as messy to make. Make thumb or finger prints of paint, ground chalk, ink, vegetable colouring, even mud. Use a pen or pencil to give the thumb-print animal his ears and tail and other features.

A TOE FILLED WITH GOLD

Long, long ago there were three sisters, each girl as sweet as a summer's day, yet not one of them could marry. In their city of Myra, the eldest daughter in a family had to be the first to marry. Only after that could her sisters wed. That was the way of things in far-off Turkey, long ago.

Now, the eldest sister did have a true love, but she couldn't marry him because she had no dowry. A dowry was very important. It was the goods and money which were always given to the bridegroom by the bride's family to help him set up house. That was another way with things in far-off Turkey, long ago. No dowry, no wedding!

There was no one who could help the sisters with their problem. Their mother and father were dead, so what was to become of them?

Then, late one afternoon, the eldest sister washed her thick woollen stockings and hung them in the fireplace to dry. They were still dangling there when the three girls went to bed.

While they slept, very late in the evening—perhaps it was midnight—a little leather bag of gold coins hurtled down the chimney, through a thickness of black soot and papery ashes. *Flump!* It dropped through the top of one stocking, lumped down the leg and nestled in the toe.

On the other side of the chimney, outside in the darkness, someone wearing a pointed hood chuckled happily before striding off quickly into the night. No one saw the man go. No one at all! No one knew where the little bag of coins had come from, but the three girls were delighted with the gift. It was enough for the eldest sister's dowry.

She married her true love. So, in due course, her younger sisters married theirs because they too received dowries in the same way: a little bag of leather coins in the toe of newly washed woollen stockings.

Each of the gifts was a wedding present from a kindly old bishop. His name was Nicholas, and nothing pleased him more than to help people secretly. However, news of some of Nicholas' deeds did become known, and that is how this story came to be told.

Ever since that time it is believed that Saint Nicholas, or Santa Claus as he's often called, comes quietly on Christmas Eve to fill the stockings of children with gifts. Traditionally, we expect him to wear a red hood trimmed with fur to keep him warm—but children in another part of the world are just as sure that he wears the tall, peaked hat of a bishop.

Bishop Nicholas' birthday was 5th December. When that time comes each year, Dutch children each leave a shoe and a bunch of carrots and some hay by the door. Then they go to bed. They know that while they sleep Saint Nicholas and his friend Peter will come riding by. The horse will eat the food and a gift will be left in the shoe.

FIND US QUICKLY IF YOU CAN

Nicholas, I beg of you,
Drop into my shoe,
Something sweet or sweeter.
Thank you, Saint and Peter!

Put your long red mantle on,
St Nicholas, good and holy man,
Drive your sleigh from Amsterdam
And find us quickly if you can.

A NICHOLAS SACK

Why not make a
sack like the
little bag
belonging
to Saint Nicholas?
You'll need a tough, thick
bag, like the one that the
groceries are carried in from the
supermarket. A little way from
the top edge thread a
string so that the sack can
be tied. Does it
need decorating?
You decide.

141

A SUPER STOCKING

A supermarket bag
can be turned by
you into a long
stocking. Or find
some thick red
paper, or material
which nobody needs.
Cut two stocking
shapes the same size.
Glue, or sew, or
staple them together.
Be sure that toes
match and heels meet
and legs match. Trim
the edges if need be.
Now turn down the top of the stocking
into a cuff. Decorate that in any way
that you like. Last of all, sew a loop
to the cuff so the stocking can be
hung up. Add some joy bells if
you have any—and that's all.

142

MEMORY GAME

The memory game can be played at any time; a very good occasion is during a long car trip, or on a train. All you need to do is to remember everything that is found in the Christmas stocking. Many things can go in, the sillier the better.

The first player says,

> "In my Christmas stocking
> there is a round red apple."

The second player says,

> "In my Christmas stocking
> there is a round red apple,
> and a big grumpy bear."

The third player says,

> "In my Christmas stocking
> there is a round red apple,
> a big grumpy bear and
> a cauliflower cushion."

And so the game goes on, passing from one player to the next. The stocking grows bigger and fatter as more things are crammed in. Make your own rules. If a forgetful person makes a mistake the game goes on without him. The winner remembers everything packed into the stocking.

A VISIT FROM ST NICHOLAS

T'was the night before Christmas, when all through the
house
Not a creature was stirring, not even a mouse:
The stockings were hung by the chimney with care,
In hopes that St Nicholas soon would be there;
The children were nestled all snug in their beds
While visions of sugar-plums danced in their heads;
And Mamma in her 'kerchief, and I in my cap,
Had just settled down for a long winter's nap,
When out on the lawn there arose such a clatter,
I sprang from my bed to see what was the matter.
Away to the window I flew like a flash,
Tore open the shutters and threw up the sash.
The moon on the breast of the new-fallen snow
Gave a lustre of midday to objects below,
When, what to my wondering eyes did appear,
But a miniature sleigh and eight tiny reindeer,
With a little old driver, so lively and quick,
I knew in a moment it must be St Nick.
More rapid than eagles his coursers they came,
And he whistled, and shouted, and called them by name:
"Now, Dasher! now, Dancer! now, Prancer and Vixen!
On, Comet, on, Cupid! on, Donder and Blitzen!
To the top of the porch! to the top of the wall!
Now dash away! dash away! dash away all!"
As dry leaves that before the wild hurricane fly,
When they meet with an obstacle, mount to the sky,
So up to the housetop the coursers they flew,
With a sleigh full of toys, and St Nicholas too.
And then, in a twinkling, I heard on the roof
The prancing and pawing of each little hoof.

144

As I drew in my head, and was turning around,
Down the chimney St Nicholas came with a bound.
He was dressed all in fur, from his head to his foot,
And his clothes were all tarnished with ashes and soot;
A bundle of toys he had flung on his back,
And he looked like a pedlar just opening his pack.
His eyes—how they twinkled! his dimples, how merry!
His cheeks were like roses, his nose like a cherry!
His droll little mouth was drawn up like a bow,
And the beard on his chin was as white as the snow;
The stump of a pipe he held tight in his teeth,
And the smoke, it encircled his head like a wreath;
He had a broad face and a round little belly
That shook, when he laughed, like a bowl full of jelly.
He was chubby and plump, a right jolly old elf,
And I laughed when I saw him, in spite of myself;
A wink of his eye and a twist of his head,
Soon gave me to know I had nothing to dread;
He spoke not a word, but went straight to his work,
And filled all the stockings; then turned with a jerk,
And laying his finger aside of his nose,
And giving a nod, up the chimney he rose.
He sprang to his sleigh, to his team gave a whistle,
And away they all flew like the down of a thistle.
But I heard his exclaim, ere he drove out of sight,

Happy Christmas to all,
And to all a good-night!"

Clement Moore

SING! DANCE!

Sing,
Dance
Whisper along the way.
What shall we whisper?
It is Christ's Day.

Sing,
Dance,
What shall we bring?
Let no hand go empty
of gifts for the king.

Sing,
Dance,
A cake baked brown and sweet,
Rosita brings
for Him to eat.

Sing,
Dance,
Miguel brings a mouse,
grey and small
for Christ's house

Sing,
Dance,
Whisper along the way.
What shall we whisper?
It is Christ's Day.

There are two saints named Stephen. St Stephen of Jerusalem was born at about the same time as the Christ Child.

St Stephen, or Steffan, of Norrala in Sweden, lived almost one thousand years ago. Both saints are honoured on the day following Christmas Day, but it is Steffan of Norrala and his five horses that these verses describe.

STEFFAN WAS A STABLE BOY

Oh, Steffan was a stable boy
And just after Christmas night
He watered his horses five,
Then followed a star's great light.

White were two of Steffan's horses
Stepping along so lightly,
They knew that they must follow too
The star that shone so brightly.

Red were two of Steffan's horses
With prancing feet so spritely,
Dancing through the night's long ride
While the snow fell down so whitely.

Grey was one of Steffan's horses
And that one carried Steffan,
He rode his grey, led they say,
By the star, above in heaven.

Oh, Steffan rode, and he rode far,
With his horses five that night.
They rode on to Bethlehem
Where they found the Baby, Christ.

Make five little horses from play dough or modelling clay, or carve them from balsa wood. Colour your horses like Steffan's. Use wool for their tails and manes.

And for a horse to ride, sit back-to-front on a chair. Push a broom through the chair rungs for the horse's tail. String, a cord, an old belt, or anything long and thin can be tied to the chair back for reins. Up you get and away you go, chair riding!

However, be sure first, that it's all right with the adults at your house to turn a chair into a horse.

Can you think of other ways to make a horse?

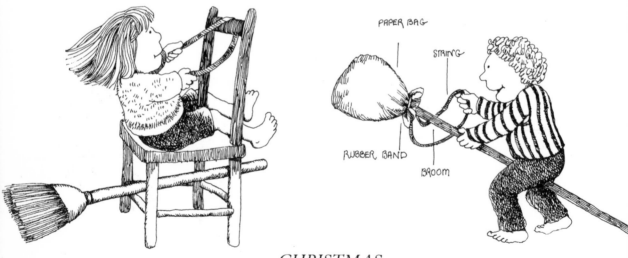

PAPER BAG
STRING
RUBBER BAND
BROOM

CHRISTMAS

The holly's up, the house is bright,
The tree is ready, the candles alight.
Rejoice . . . and be glad
All children tonight!

Peter Cornelius

THE DAY AFTER CHRISTMAS

Before castles were built from stone, at a time when kings lived in towers of wood, there was once a goodly king named Wenceslas. He knelt down and said his prayers each morning and night. He went to church. He kept the holy days. And the day after Christmas each year he celebrated with a feast in honour of St Stephen.

One of these feasts was held during the worst winter men had known for a long, long time. All through the day wind whined about the tower. It pushed at the door, rattled the window shutters and piled snow against the tower walls. Sometimes it blew through chinks in the timbers to swirl smoke and scatter ash from the great log fire over the king's guests. They wiped their eyes and coughed, and went on drinking and eating, singing and talking and arguing. It was noisy and crowded in the hall of the tower.

By the afternoon, Wenceslas had tired of the laughter and noise. He moved to a window and pulled aside the shutter to look out down his hillside. Fresh snow had fallen, blanketing it in whiteness. Deep, crisp, even snow, unmarked except for a crooked line of deep holes which had been left by a man's footsteps. That man was still walking away from the tower. His back was bent in a bow by a bundle across his thin shoulders.

"Who is that?" asked the King. "Who is that man? What is he doing abroad on such a day?"

A page scurried to the window. "It's only a peasant, Sire," he said. "He's someone from out near the Fountain of St Agnes."

"That's close by the forest," said the King. "It is far off. What brings him here? Should he not be at home feasting with his family?"

"He wouldn't have much for a feast, Sire," answered the page. "He is looking for fuel, I'd say. He's been searching for sticks to keep his hut warm, I suppose. He's sure to have children there, Sire."

"Yes," said the King thoughtfully as he fastened the shutter across the slit of a window. "If the man has come so far to find fuel his stomach may be empty too." Wenceslas turned to the page. "Run to the table, lad, and bring me meat and wine. Then fetch me some pine logs. And after that, my boots and cloak."

"But, Sire!"

"Hurry, lad, so I may go to the peasant's hut."

Perhaps others offered to go in the King's stead, but in the end it was only the page who set out with King Wenceslas to walk to the forest. Burdened with the fuel and food they stepped into the wind.

150

It whipped their cloaks, twisting and winding the woollen material about their bodies. It threw showers of snow at their faces, stinging their cheeks and eyes. It scudded clouds across the moon, darkening their way. And it pushed and pulled at them and threw them down into drifts of snow. Their limbs stiffened and their numbed hands cramped about their bundles. And after a while, the King silently took the boy's burdens and carried them with his own.

Then the lad became too weary to go any farther. "Leave me," he told the King. "I cannot go on." His knees crumpled and he sank down into the snow.

Wenceslas dragged the boy to his feet. "*You will follow me,*" he said. "Walk in my footsteps. Walk behind me as I order you."

The boy seemed unable to move. He stared at the King.

"Obey me!" shouted Wenceslas; and he walked on, ploughing a way through the snow for the boy to follow.

And so they reached the peasant's hut. Had the boy stayed behind he would have frozen to death. We have been told no more of Wenceslas and his page on that St Stephen's Day. How did the poor man feel when his king brought him food and fuel? What did he do? And were there children in his hut? Perhaps you could end the story for yourself.

We do know that Wenceslas lived to do so many kind deeds that his people built a cathedral in his honour . . . long ago at a time when kings lived in towers made from wood.

The day after Christmas, St Stephen's Day, was when masters once gave presents to their servants, and handed out gifts to the butcher and other tradesmen who had served them well through the year.

Today, it is the postman and the dustman and the milkman who are likely to receive small presents, usually before Christmas Day.

Lucky children may be taken to the theatre to watch a pantomime. With fun and nonsense, actors and actresses bring to life an old fairytale. It may be *Cinderella.* A girl plays the part of Prince Charming and two clumsy men are the ugly sisters. Or maybe the day after Christmas brings the treat of going to a ballet, to see a story told through dance and music. No words are spoken, not one. Often the story of the ballet is an old favourite. Perhaps you've heard the story of the Nutcracker before. Perhaps you've seen the ballet. Sometimes the little girl is called Clare. Sometimes she is Marie.

THE NUTCRACKER

It began when Dr Drosselmayer gave his little god-daughter a wooden nutcracker as a Christmas present. Clara had no idea that it was enchanted. The nutcracker looked very much like any other nutcracker, in that it was just big enough to fit comfortably into her hand, and it was carved from a pale wood. But it was shaped like a strange young prince. Usually nutcrackers were more likely to be carved as a cranky old man, or a snapping dragon, or a knobbled crocodile with clenched jaws.

Clara was delighted with her prince, and she carried the nutcracker about with her. She even took it to the Christmas party she was sharing with her small brother and their friends.

Fritz noticed how often his sister stopped to look at her present. And what with the party's excitement and staying up later than his usual bedtime, Fritz became very silly. All at once he snatched the nutcracker from Clara's hands. When she tried to take it back, teasing little Fritz giggled and flung it across the room. It flew over a small girl's head. It spun over a couch and dropped somewhere on the floor.

"Clara! Clara!" the children's mother called to her. She hadn't seen what had happened and wanted Clara to help serve the party food. For the time being Clara had to leave the nutcracker where it was. It was still under the couch when the party ended and the guests went home. It was still there when Clara and Fritz went to bed, but Clara had not forgotten her gift. "I'll fetch it before Fritz can get his hands on it again," she told herself as she hopped out of bed and sped back down the stairs to the drawing-room.

Clara expected the big room to be dark with shadows as she pushed open the door. Instead, it was ablaze with light. Now that the guests were gone, the Christmas tree looked taller than Clara remembered it. Its topmost branch was brushing against the ceiling.

She slipped by the tree, running lightly on her toes to the couch. The nutcracker was still there. Bending down, she fished it out. It, too, seemed strangely larger than when she had last seen it. Clara turned it about, glad to find that it wasn't damaged much by the fall. Surely it wasn't growing bigger? Clara wondered if she were dreaming.

The nutcracker was growing. It grew tall and slim. And as it grew the wooden carving faded . . . faded. The next moment an elegant prince bowed before the little girl. Clara had released him from a binding spell. And as the prince began to thank her, a horde of grey mice trampled through the door to invade the drawing-room. They were led by an enormous mouse king. He barred his teeth. He brandished a sword. He threatened Clara and the prince.

The prince leapt before Clara, protecting her from the advancing mice. Snarling and shrilling, they rushed upon them, cornering the prince and the little girl. Then the mouse king signalled the attack by striking out at the prince.

As he thrust forward, at that moment, as if obeying a silent call for aid, there was a clatter of boots, the sound of trumpets and the rat-a-tat of drums. And out of a box left by Fritz under the Christmas tree tumbled an army of toy soldiers. No sooner did the toys land on the carpet than they were changed to man-sized dragoons who charged the monster mice.

Valiantly the Nutcracker Prince struggled with the ferocious mouse king. It was a hard battle. Brave as he was, Clara saw that her prince was weakening. She was fearful for his life and flew to his side, dragging off her slipper as she ran. *Whack!* Clara struck at the mouse. Down he went. He was dead.

The battle ended. The mouse army fled. They scuttled from the room, carrying away their king with them. And as they left, the last of the spell enchanting the prince was broken. He could return to his own land, and he invited Clara to travel there with him.

Taking her hand, he led her to the Christmas tree, where he stood with his arms outstretched.

And now the tree seemed to grow taller still. Up and up it stretched beyond the ceiling, to become a giant forest pine. Moonlight shimmered and faded, shimmered and faded as a gauze of silvered mist curtained the tree. Clara

I CAN BE AS TALL AS A CHRISTMAS TREE

felt that she too was wrapped in mist and moonlight . . . and then she was floating in a walnut boat over banks covered with snow. The drawing-room was gone. Above her, below her, light as fragile snowflakes, swirled a welcoming band of snow fairies, dancing to the music of the wind.

Clara had reached the Nutcracker Prince's Kingdom of the Sweets, a sugar-plum land where houses were made from chocolate and peppermint sticks, where hills were almond rocks and caves were hollowed honeycomb. There were lollypop trees and candied flowers, and a glittering palace built from sugar. Here the Sugar-plum Fairy reigned from a golden throne of honey sweets.

The Sugar-plum Fairy heard of Clara's bravery during the battle with the mice and she rewarded the little girl with sights she would never forget. Seating Clara upon her own throne she summoned together the people of Sugar-plum Land.

If you see the ballet, like Clara you will meet the makers of every kind of sugar-plum. Chinese dancers toddle with their huge teapot, bronzed Arabians dance with coffee cups, wild Cossacks kick and twirl. More and more dancers enchanted Clara. Then the Sugar-plum Fairy herself danced with the Nutcracker Prince. Soon everyone joined in, and Clara danced too.

And afterwards, when Clara returned home, she never could be sure whether or not it had all been a dream.

CHRISTMAS BOXES

The day after Christmas is no longer known as St Stephen's Day. It is usually called Boxing Day. Often it is a holiday.

Perhaps Boxing Day has always been a tidy-up-clean-up-putting-away day after the fun of Christmas Day, but its name may have come about for a different reason. People had spoken of Christmas boxes for hundreds of years. They meant gifts of money.

The first Christmas boxes were fat little pigs made from clay and they were given to children. Along the back of each pig was a narrow slit, just big enough to slip a coin through. When the piggy bank was rattle-full of money it was smashed open.

PIGGY BANK

There isn't any need to break open a piggy bank if it is made from a short plastic bottle. It will need a slit to bank the money, and a grown-up will help there. Or the coins can be put in through the neck of the bottle. Block it off with a cork if the bottle doesn't have a screw cap. The cap or cork is the pig's nose as well. Glue on four cork feet. Now give the pig some eyes and ears cut from sticky tape. Add a pipe-cleaner tail and decorate his body with sticky tape.

A small tin with a tightly fitted lid can be turned into an animal bank. Ask someone to make a slit in the lid for you. Take off the label by soaking the tin in water for a little while.

If you are making a pig, give him a nose from an egg-carton cup. Fix it on with masking tape. Give him ears from paper, felt, velvet or cardboard. Fix them with masking tape, too. Your pig needs painting. What about a pink pig? Or a striped one? A spotted pig? A flowered pig? When the paint dries, finish off his face with slanted piggy-wig eyes and a curled up mouth. Draw these on, or use paper, or glued buttons.

A cat money-box needs a smaller button-round nose. Find something to make that. Cut a piece from an egg-box cup if you can't find something better. And a cat has pointed ears and whiskers. Borrow some straws from the broom for the whiskers.

What other animals can you make into a money-box?

COULD IT BE?

Here is the box
Make your hand into a fist.
Put on the lid
Cover it with the other hand.
I wonder whatever inside it is hid
Peek under the lid, by lifting
your palm a little.
Could it be?
Take another look.
Yes, without doubt
And another peep.
Open the box and let it come out
Open up your fist. You could
hide a sweet or a tiny toy in
your hand if you like, or else
nothing at all!

SLIP! SLIDE! SWOOOOOSH!

Like many other small bears, Fred was a great one for sliding and slipping and tumbling about. The best slide he ever had was in a cardboard box which he found upside-down bottom-up on a hillside. It was the kind of box which groceries are often packed into at the supermarket, but Fred didn't know that. On the sides of the box was written *Christmas Cakes—Special,* but Fred couldn't read. He took a good look at the box. Then he sniffed it. Then he pawed at it, touching and patting it until it flipped over, right-way-up, bottom-down. "Ahh! This is something to put my foot in," said Fred.

It was not. When Fred put his foot in he couldn't walk.

It wasn't nice to eat, either. When he bit at the box it tasted dry and papery.

So Fred put it on his head. It dropped over his eyes, over his ears, over his nose and Fred couldn't see where he was. He wobbled about. The box toppled off his head. Fred fell down too, to land seat-first in the box.

"Hey!" shouted Foxy running up the hill. "What have you got there?"

Fred leaned forward to see who had shouted and . . . slip . . .slide. . .*swooooosh!* Away down the grass whizzed Fred in the box. *Whee!*

"It's something to slide in!" Fred shouted to Foxy.

And it was the best slide he'd ever had. Woops! At the bottom of the grassy slope Fred tumbled out of the box, then, pulling it behind him, padded up the hill again.

"That was a grand slide," said Foxy. "May I have a go?"

"Yes, hop in," said Fred.

They both sat in the box. Slip . . . slide . . . *swooooosh!* Away down the grass they whizzed. Woops! At the bottom of the grassy slope Fred tumbled out; then, pulling Foxy in the box, he pad-padded up the hill again.

At the top Foxy's brothers sat looking and waiting. "We want to go too," they said.

"All right! Hop in!" said Fred.

They all squeezed in the box. Slip . . . slide . . . *swooooosh!* Away down the grass they whizzed. Woops! At the bottom of the grassy slope Fred tumbled out, and then, pulling Foxy and his brothers in the box, he pad, pad, padded up the hill again.

At the top Bird sat looking and waiting. "May I have a go?" she asked.

"Hop in!" said Fred.

It was such a tight squeeze in the box there really wasn't room for Bird. She sat on Foxy's shoulder. Slip . . . *slide . . . swooooosh!* Away down the grass they whizzed. At the bottom Fred fell out again, then pulling Foxy *and* his brothers *and* Bird in the box, he pad . . . pad . . . padded up the hill again.

At the top Butterfly was looking and waiting. "Is there room for me?" she asked.

"Yes, if you can find somewhere to sit," Fred told her. "Bird had to sit on Foxy's shoulder."

Butterfly settled on Foxy's nose. *Slip. . .slide. . .swooooosh!* They skimmed down the grass. At the bottom Fred bounced out once more, then, pulling Foxy *and* his brothers *and* Bird *and* Butterfly, he pad . . . pad . . . padded half-way up the hill. "Phew!" he sighed, and sat down where he was.

"Come on, Fred!" said the others. "Get up! Pull us up! We want another slide. What's up! Get going now!"

"I can't. I'm too tired," said Fred.

"Then we'll pull *you* up."

They bundled Fred into the box. Pulling and pushing, they shoved him up the hill. Then everyone squeezed in for another slide. They slid and slipped and slid. Everyone helped to pull the box now—that is, until it wore out. No more slides after that. But perhaps they found another box to play with on another day.

NEW YEAR

God be here, God be there,
We wish you all a happy year;
God without, God within,
Let the old year out and the New Year in.

The sixth day after Christmas is New Year's Eve. It is the
end of the old year. At midnight the new year begins. Just
about everywhere, people welcome the new year in ways
which are special to them. Mostly it is very noisy. Church
bells ring. People laugh and sing and wish each other a happy
year. Hooters and whistles screech, clappers rattle, sirens
whoop and fireworks explode.

Quarrels are mended; often people make promises (which
they call 'resolutions') to be better. Many resolutions are too
hard to keep and they become forgotten until the next new
year comes.

Some people smash glasses and plates. Others clean their
houses from floors to ceilings.

In Scotland, the day and night are called Hogmanay.
Hogmanay is the best time of the year, Scottish folk say.
There are presents and parties and singing and dancing.
When the clock strikes twelve the front door is thrown open
to welcome in the new year. The first person to step inside
the house should be a dark-haired man. He is supposed to
bring good luck to the family.

Scottish children have their own celebrations. On New
Year's Eve little groups dress up in old sheets and troop from
house to house, singing:

> "Come out, good Wife,
> And give us cake,
> None of your grey
> But newly baked."

The good-natured housewife gives the children some of
her New Year baking. Some buttery shortbread maybe, or
slices of bun. Or maybe a handful of nuts or sweets.

164

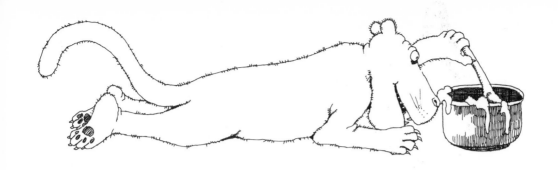

SHORTBREAD

Put into a bowl *2 cups of flour* with ½ *cup of sugar* and a pinch of salt. Icing sugar or fine caster sugar are better than ordinary sugar.

Now soften *1 cup of butter* and add it to the bowl. Work it and work it into the other ingredients. Use a spoon or clean fingers.

Knead it on a floured board, then roll it and cut it and prick it with a fork.

Bake your shortbread at 300° for about 30 minutes, or until it is just touched with colour.

It should be crisp and buttery and delicious to eat.

HOGMANAY CAKE

In a certain part of Scotland at one time there were some wee fairy folk. They may be there yet, for all I know. They were as slender as grass blades and quicker than the wind and they all liked nothing better than to get hold of a piece of home-made cake. Not much of it came their way. Just a few crumbs now and again, and only if they were quick enough to snatch those up before a housewife shook her tablecloth, or a granny washed the cake plates.

A great longing for cake grew upon the wee folk. Their mouths watered for it, but they hadn't the smallest notion of how to make cake for themselves. Then came one Hogmanay . . . and they made up their minds to have a feast of cake. And to make sure of their cake, they carried off the best cook in all Scotland. She was called Katie.

Katie was walking along a path on her way to the laird's big house where she was to bake the cakes for his Hogmanay party. In one hand she was swinging her kittie-bag, and inside it were her starched white apron and her wooden spoons. She was waving her other hand about her head, thinking she was brushing off some pesty insects. *Buzz-buzz!* They were annoying, darting about her face like that. Little did Katie know that it was the wee folk flitting close to toss fern-seed in her eyes. And the next thing, before Katie could draw another breath, she was magicked off to the wee folks' place.

166

She knew where she was the instant she landed there. She knew, too, that she'd be lucky if she ever left that fairy place. The wee folk always tried to keep their visitors for ever. No one could rescue her, because not a soul knew where the wee folk lived. And here they were, clamouring about her knees, crowding and jostling and demanding that she should make them a cake for Hogmanay. Ah, perhaps she could trick them by making the cake they were pestering her for!

"You poor wee things!" Katie told them. "Of course I'll make you a cake. I will, I will. Hasn't anyone ever thought to make you a cake before this?" And as she spoke she untied her kittie-bag to put on her big white apron. "You shall have your cake, just as soon as you fetch me some flour. Have you any fine white flour?"

Flour? The wee folk never used flour. Never!

"Then you must flit to my house and bring back the sack of flour that's under my kitchen table," she said.

Lightning-quick the fairies whisked off to fetch the flour. It was a heavy load but back they came with it.

Katie was pleased, but then she sent them back to her house to bring some butter.

Then she wanted sugar.

Next, she needed eggs.

After that, she must have milk.

By now the wee folk were plum worn-out with the flitting and the flying and the carrying of heavy loads. It was only the thought of their Hogmanay cake which kept them going, and now that Katie had all the ingredients they hoped for a rest. But here she was wanting a mixing bowl.

The biggest bowl that the wee folk could find was about tea-cup size, and a small fragile cup at that. It just would not do. "Back to my house with you," shooed Katie. "You'll find my big yellow bowl on the shelf in the kitchen. Bring that back so I can get on with the cake. Don't break it, now."

They flapped back with the bowl and then to their despair Kate said, "Ouch! I've forgotten my egg whisk."

And egg whisk she got. The wee folk were so exhausted they crumpled into little heaps on the floor. They had never worked so hard for anything: but the big buttery Hogmanay cake was worth their efforts.

They watched Katie beating the butter and sugar to a fluffy cream. Round and over swung her big wooden spoon. Round and over, and the wee folks' eyes greedily followed the spoon. Round and over!

Then, all at once, Katie stopped beating. She sighed. "Aoaaah, it's just no use me trying to cook. I miss my little puss-cat. He always sits by my right foot while I bake."

Whisk! The wee folk skimmed off and away again, then back to Katie with her little puss-cat. He sat at her feet and purred. She beat the sugar and butter again. Round and over! Round and over!

Suddenly the beating stopped and Katie was sighing again, Och! It's not my best cooking that I'll do today. I miss my little puppy-dog too much. He always sits by my left foot and snores while I bake."

Whisk! The wee folk were gone, then back they came again with Katie's little puppy-dog. He lay at her feet and snored. And Katie broke eggs into the bowl and whipped and whipped them into the batter. Plosh-plosh! Plosh-plosh!

Once again the beating stopped and Katie sighed. "Och! It's me wee bairn! I can't finish this cake while he cries at home for his porridge. Long past his feeding time it is."

So the wee folk fetched the wee baby and his cradle and all to Katie. Her baby was crying, roaring and bellowing as a healthy hungry bairn will. The wee folk didn't like his noise. Katie was quick to see that it worried them and she said, "It's as I thought, he's hungry, poor lambie! Bring his Dadda to keep him quiet. I must get on with the cake. There's been interruptions enough."

Well, the wee folk were not giving up their cake now. They were tired enought to faint, but fetch the baby's Dadda they did. The poor man rubbed his eyes in amazement, hardly believing what he could see. There was Katie, his dear wife, beating a bowl of batter like fury. There was their purring cat and their snoring dog and their howling baby. The place was in an uproar, and as Katie bent across to give the bairn a wooden spoon to bang she whispered to her man, "Prod the dog, otherwise we'll be here forever."

And prod the dog he did.

The dog yelped and bit the cat.

The cat yowled.

The baby howled and banged the spoon.

And Katie beat the batter.

The noise was outrageous. The wee folk were distracted. They covered their ears and crowded together, flitting about bumping into each other and Katie. They hated the noise, but somehow they must bear it to get their Hogmanay cake.

Then the cat stopped yowling.

The man trod on its tail to set it off again, and soon Katie was shouting over the din, "The cake is ready to be baked. *Where . . . is . . . the . . . oven?*"

Oven? The wee folk had no oven.

"Then I shall just have to take the cake home and bake it," said Katie. "We can't waste good batter."

"Take it and keep it," shrilled the wee folk. "And take your noisy lot with you!" They couldn't stand the racket any longer. Not even Hogmanay cake was worth such sore ears. And they wished Katie away.

She carried home the cake and popped it in her oven. Then she fed porridge to the bairn, who was soon smiling. She fed cream to the cat, who was soon purring. She gave the dog lots of bones with meat still on them, and that made him wag his tail.

Then Katie took herself off to the laird's house where she'd been going in the first place. On the way, along the path behind a rock, she left a big round buttery Hogmanay cake. The wee folk smelt it. They took it to their place and had a Hogmanay party.

In the same place the following week, Katie left another cake. She left cake there as long as she lived. Sometimes it was wheaten cake. Sometimes it was girdle cake. Sometimes it was shortbread or sticky buns or something else.

The wee folk were grateful. Katie was the best cook in all of Scotland, so they sometimes left her a little bag of gold—none of that rubbishy fairy gold, mind you, but honest-to-goodness round metal coins. There was never enough to make Katie rich, but plenty to spare to pay for the baking.

TICK-TOCK!

Tick - tock! Hear the clock!

Tick out the old year, Tock in the new.

ALL IN THE MORNING

It was on the Twelfth Day,
And all in the morning,
The wise men were led
To our heavn'ly King;
And was this not a joyful thing?
And sweet Jesus they called Him by name.

It was on the Twentieth Day,
And all in the morning,
The wise men returned
From our heav'nly King:
And was this not a joyful thing?
And sweet Jesus they called Him by name.

TWELFTH NIGHT SONG

See them! There they go,
Three great kings go riding through snow,
Three kings on three horses
Go riding on their way
To see Him, Jesu, born a king today.

Drums beat as they come,
Joyfully riding to see Mary's son,
The new-born King.
To Bethlehem they come to see Him,
Jesu, Mary's new-born son.

Furs they brought the Child,
Furs warm and soft, from forest wild,
And gay songs to sing,
To Him they did bring, to Him, to Jesu,
Tiny little sweet boy Child.

174

TWELFTH NIGHT

The twelfth day after Christmas is the Feast of Epiphany. Epiphany is an old word which means *the showing.*

We are told that the three Wise Men, led by the great star, came to Bethlehem on Twelfth Night. They carried precious gifts for the Christ Child, and Mary showed them the Baby they had travelled so far to find.

Epiphany marks the end of the Christmas celebrations. It is time to take down the Christmas tree and to pack away the decorations for another year.

Once, people ended their Christmas with yet another party, a Twelfth Night party. A special cake was served. Before it was baked, a dried bean and a dried pea were slipped into the mixture. The one to find the bean in his slice became the King of Fools until midnight. Whoever discovered the pea was his queen. They wore paper crowns and set their party "subjects" all kinds of nonsense tasks.

At one such party, in a king's banqueting hall, a very magnificent pie was served instead of the cake. And when the pie crust was cut, birds began to sing. They flew out of the pie, fluttering about the candles and the guests. And that was the beginning of—

SING A SONG OF SIXPENCE

Sing a song of sixpence,
    A pocket full of rye;
Four-and-twenty blackbirds
    Baked in a pie.

When the pie was opened,
    The birds began to sing;
Was not that a dainty dish,
    To set before the king?

The king was in his counting-house,
    Counting out his money;
The queen was in the parlour,
    Eating bread and honey.

The maid was in the garden,
    Hanging out the clothes,
When down came a blackbird
    And pecked off her nose.

She went to the doctor
    To get a wooden nose,
And when she came home again
    She couldn't smell a rose!

You may know a different ending to the rhyme. Children have known about that blackbird pie for more than two hundred years. It was a pie to remember!

Other things happened on Twelfth Night. Sometimes small gifts were exchanged, in memory of the gifts given to the baby, Jesus, on the first Twelfth Night.

And today, there are small children in Spain who know that the Three Wise Men will pass their way and leave small gifts in their shoes.

Other children know that an old friend called Baboushka will call on them while they sleep and leave small presents.

176

BABOUSHKA

All day and every day Baboushka cooked and swept and washed and stitched. Most of the time she was singing, making up her own songs when she'd sung all those she knew. Baboushka was round and plump and cheerful and she lived alone in a forest. Few people came to see her. Her house was well away from the road.

She was surprised one afternoon to hear twigs a-snapping and hard snow a-crackling. Who was coming? Was it a bear?

Baboushka listened.

No! That wasn't a bear. A bear would be quieter in the snow.

Tramp-tramp-tramp! People were walking in the snow. Visitors were coming to her house!

Baboushka pulled aside a curtain, but she couldn't see anyone. She hurried to the fire and threw on more logs. She straightened her hair and pulled off her apron. She was ready for the visitors. And just in time! There was a hard knock on the door. The single knock made Baboushka feel a little afraid. "Who's t-t-there?" she asked timidly in a small thin cracked voice. "W-who knocks on my door?"

177

"Travellers," a tired voice answered. "Travellers, and we are lost. Could you please help us find the road?"

Such a pleasant voice could only belong to a kind man, Baboushka thought. "Come in and rest by my fire," she said as she opened the door. "It is a cold raw day to be out."

"Thank you!" said a young man. He led an old man over the doorstep and into the room. Behind them was a third person, shaking the snow from his shoulders and stamping his feet.

Baboushka looked at the travellers. The young man was fair, the other was old and grey. The third man was tall and dark-skinned. Their clothes were rich silks and furs, as fine as any king's. But kings or not, they needed to be warmed by the fire and nourished with Baboushka's good thick broth.

She bustled about pouring the broth into wooden bowls, then finding spoons and bread. And while she worked, they told her that they were journeying, seeking a baby prince. "We have followed His star," they said, "but it is hidden now by snow clouds. And we have lost our way."

"After you have eaten and rested I'll show you to the road," promised Baboushka. "You'll not need the star once you're on the road again."

"But it is His star. Only His star can lead us to the Christ Child," they explained.

"Christ Child?" asked Baboushka. "What Child is this? A child with a star! The stars belong to the sky."

So the three men told Baboushka all they knew of the holy Child and how His star was a sign of His birth. They showed her the gifts they were taking to Him and she clasped her hands in wonder. "I wish I had seen His star. If only I could visit Him too," she said.

I LOVE VISITORS VISITING ME!

"Then come with us, Baboushka! Come with us to find the Child."

"No, no, no! I'm too old." Baboushka shook her head. "My creaking old bones are not used to travelling, but I will show you on your way."

Baboushka took the three men through the forest to the road. Then she returned to her house, where there was no broth left to warm her. She sat by her fire, rocking backwards and forwards in her chair, wishing aloud. "I would have liked to have looked upon the Christ Child," she said over and over again. Later she said, "Perhaps I could go? Yes, in the morning! Yes, I will go. I will follow the travellers and find the Babe."

At once she began to get ready for the journey. Into a pack she put some treasured things, little things which children like to keep. A little wooden horse, some painted pine-cones, a bright feather, a coloured stone, a knitted ball and a soft doll made from rags and straw.

In the morning, she tied a scarf on her head, locked her door and set off into the snow. New snow had fallen, covering the travellers' footsteps. Baboushka didn't know which way they had gone. "Have you seen three men dressed like kings?" she asked a farmer.

"Kings don't go out walking in this weather!" snorted the farmer, and he walked on.

"Have you seen a bright star in the sky?" Baboushka asked a shepherd.

"Of course! Hundreds of stars every night. Each one is as bright as its neighbour," answered the shepherd; and chuckling to himself, he went off as fast as he could.

"Do you know where is the Child born to be king?"
Baboushka asked a herdsman.

"Don't ask me!" snapped the herdsman. "Babies are born
every day hereabouts. None of them will be a king!" And he
turned on his heel and away he went.

Baboushka walked for the rest of the day. She wandered to
many more places, meeting many more people and always
asking for the Christ Child. No one could tell her where to
find the baby. She did find, however, as she travelled about,
some small unhappy children, and children who were tired
and sick. Baboushka comforted them with a small toy from
her pack. And they gave her smiles in thanks.

Ever since, Baboushka has gone on looking for the Christ
child, travelling all over her country.

On Twelfth Night, twelve days after Christmas, she
leaves the children there a small gift. Perhaps you have heard
of Baboushka? Or, as she is sometimes called, Befana.

BABOUSHKA DOLL

Plump little Baboushka is often carved from wood as a doll. Take off her head and there's another doll inside . . . and another. The last one may be as small as your thumb.

One Baboushka doll, just one, can be made from a plastic cream jar, or one that is a similar squat shape.

Make her head by glueing a styro foam ball, or a ping-pong ball to the top of the bottle. Or use a ball of cotton wool covered with a paper tissue, or a scrap of cloth. Push it into the neck of the bottle.

Baboushka needs a face. Paint or draw it on.

She needs a scarf. A bright piece of material will do, or use a paper tissue or a paper dishcloth.

A shawl comes next. Find something to tie about her shoulders as a shawl.

If you think she needs feet, paste on two small half-circles of dark paper, or draw them with a felt pen.

Now Baboushka is ready to go travelling, or to do whatever you have planned for her.

GOODBYE! AND HAPPY CHRISTMAS

You'll remember that Christmas was once celebrated for twelve days and nights.

On Christmas Eve the house was decorated with holly and evergreens and a huge log was dragged into the fireplace to burn through the celebrations. It was a Yule Log. In some places the fire was kindled with a piece of last year's log which had been saved for twelve months. And there was an old chant to accompany the ceremony of lighting the fire:

Fire, beautiful fire!
Log, beautiful log!
Gather us around you for this feast,
And warm us from the hearth,
And if, next year, there are not more of us,
Then, at least, let us not be fewer!

It was years later that Christmas trees were brought into houses and decorated on Christmas Eve.

Sometimes gifts were given and received on each of the twelve days of Christmas. The traditional English song *The Twelve Days of Christmas* is based on this custom. Do you recall the list of gifts?

A partridge in a pear-tree,
Two turtle doves,
Three French hens,
Four colly birds,
Five gold rings,
Six geese a-laying,
Seven swans a-swimming,
Eight maids a-milking,
nine drummers drumming,
Ten pipers piping,
Eleven ladies dancing,
Twelve lords a-leaping.

A PARTRIDGE IN A PEAR-TREE

A partridge in a pear-tree mobile is made from scrap papers, glitter, sequins if you have any, crayons or paint and a long nylon thread.

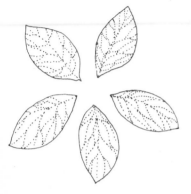

Cut five leaves from paper. Colour and decorate them.

Cut out the shapes of two partridges. Colour each bird and decorate it with glitter and sequins. Later, the two birds will be glued together to make one— tails must meet tails and beaks meet beaks. So before you start decorating, place the bird shapes so that their heads are facing each other. That will save mistakes.

Perhaps you have some feathers to make into wings and tails.

Now, cut out two pear shapes, including two small leaves as if they are sprouting from the pears. Colour the pears and the leaves. Sprinkle them with glitter too, if you like the idea of that.

When the shapes are dry you can put the mobile together.

Spread out one pear shape and a bird, *wrong* side up.

Brush both with glue.
Put the long thread of nylon on the glued pear.
Leave a space along the thread, then lay it over the partridge.
Keep the long free end of the thread well away from the paper shapes, so that it won't be in danger of being glugged up with glue.
Press the second pear on top of the thread, to cover the first pear.
Press the second bird over the thread and the first bird.
Leave the mobile to dry. Be patient! It won't take long.
When it is dry make a knot in the thread above the partridge, leaving, if you can, about the same space as you have between the pear and the bird.
Directly above the knot sew the leaves into a circle. Make another knot on top of the five leaves to keep them in position, or sew on a bright bead.
Leave the rest of the thread hanging loosely so that you can use it to hang the mobile somewhere as a Christmas greeting.

In France a similar song is called *The Year's Gifts.* There is a present for each month of the year: one partridge, two turtle doves, three wood-pigeons, four ducks flying, five rabbits trotting, six hares a-field, seven hounds running, eight shorn sheep, nine horned oxen, ten good turkeys, eleven good hams and twelve small cheeses.

And in Scotland,

the king sent gifts to his lady:
The king sent his lady on the first Yule day,
A popingo-aye (a parrot)
Who learns my carol and carries it away.

After that he sent three partridges, three plovers, a goose that was grey, three starlings, three goldspinks, a bull that was brown, three ducks a-merry laying, three swans a-merry swimming, an Arabian baboon, three hinds a-merry hunting, three maids a-merry dancing, and three stalks o'merry corn.

COME AGAIN:

Noel is leaving us,
Sad 'tis to tell,
But he will come again,
Goodbye, Noel.

The kings ride away
In the snow and the rain,
After twelve months
We shall see them again.

A ROUND OF BELLS

Christ-mas bells sound-ing so loud and so clear,

Ring-ing their mes-sage for all men to hear.

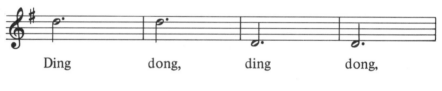

Ding dong, ding dong,

ding dong, ding dong.

Let everyone join in, one after the other, passing the song on to a neighbour and everyone having a good sing. The first singer starts off alone, singing to the end of the first line. Now the second singer begins the song anew, while the first singer continues. The song goes on and on and on as more people join in. Will it sound a screeching jangled mess? Try it and find out what it does sound like. You'll enjoy it as much as English carol singers have done for years. Tinkle bells as you sing your welcome to Christmas.

INDEX

All in the Morning	173
Baboushka	177
Baboushka Doll	182
Bells to Make	70
Bird Tree	50
Birthday Gift	23
Blow the Trumpet	14
Bonbons to Make	103
Bread and Milk	48
Bright Star, Light Star, Make a Star	31
Catch the Bell-Ringer	66
Christmas	148
Christmas Boxes	157
Christmas in Two Lands	59
Christmas Pudding	107
Come Again	187
Could It Be?	159
Crèche to Make, A	20
Day After Christmas, The	149
Decision	98
Decorations to Make	89
Eat Well! Sleep Well!	40
Find Us Quickly If You Can	141
First Christmas, The	16
Flour Paste	23
Fruity Percy	112
Games to Play	104
Gathering Stars	33
Gingerbread Man, The	90
Good Time is Coming, A	11
Goodies to Make	95
Guiding Star	27
Hogmanay Cake	166
I Wish You a Merry Christmas	130
If Wishes were Horses	81
In-a-Minute Puppets	42
Jack Horner's Plum	102
Jolly Smiling Cook	94
Julklapp!	84
Lamb of Bethlehem, A	35
Lamb to Make, A	38
Little Jack Horner	102
Little Juggler of Chartres, The	60
Little Plum Duff	108
Long, Long Ago	26
Lucky Wishbones	81
Memory Game	143
Music While You Sing	11
Nasty Little Beasties	119
New Year	163
Nicholas Sack, A	141
Nisse Finger-Puppet	41
Nutcracker, The	153
Old Donkey and Ox and Little Grey Sheep	39
On a Blue Hill	34
Paper and Cards to Make	121
Parcel	83
Partridge in a Pear Tree, A	184
Party, The	91
Piggy Bank	157
Pink Sugar Mouse	133
Play Dough	89
Plum Game, The	102
Pudding to Make, A	112
Red Cap, The	113
Remember the Birds	49
Ring of Angels to Make, A	126
Rings on Each Finger	44
Ritsch, Ratsch, Filibom!	58
Robin's Red Breast	46
Round of Bells, A	188
St Thomas' Day is Past and Gone	101
Secret, The	127
Shall I Tell You?	45
Shepherds, The	24
Shepherds to Make	26
Shortbread	165
Silvery Spidery Tree	51
Sing a Song of Sixpence	176
Sing! Dance!	146
Sing Joy	13
Sing, Sing	106
Sky High Pie	99
Slip! Slide! Swooooosh!	160
Snowflakes Falling	120
Snowflakes to Make	120
Some Presents to Make	131
Star-Light, Star-Bright	82
Steffan Was a Stable Boy	147
Sticky-Stick Puppets	44
Sugar and Spice and Little Pink Mice	137
Super Stocking, A	142
This is the Church	65
Three Kings to Make	30
Thumb Mouse	138
Tick-Tock!	173
Toe Filled with Gold, A	139
Trees to Make	54
Twelfth Night	175
Twelfth Night Song	174
Visit From St Nicholas, A	144
Walnuts and Matches	90
Wash the Dishes	83
Way of Wishes, The	74
Welcome	73
Who Remembered Joanna?	67
Wishing Harp	82

GOODBYE AND HAPPY CHRISTMAS

Now when Jesus was born in Bethlehem of Judea in the days of Herod the king, behold, there came wise men from the east to Jerusalem, saying, Where is he that is born King of the Jews? For we have seen his star in the east, and are come to worship him. When Herod the king had heard these things, he was troubled, and all Jerusalem with him. And when he had gathered all the chief priests and scribes of the people together, he demanded of them where Christ should be born. And they said unto him, In Bethlehem of Judea: for thus it is written by the prophet, And thou Bethlehem, in the land of Juda, art not the least among the princes of Juda: for out of thee shall come a governor, that shall rule my people Israel. Then Herod, when he had privily called the wise men, enquired of them diligently

what time the star appeared. And he sent them to Bethlehem, and said, Go and search diligently for the young child; and when ye have found him, bring me word again, that I may come and worship him also. When they had heard the king, they departed; and, lo, the star, which they saw in the east, went before them, till it came and stood over where the young child was. When they saw the star, they rejoiced with exceeding great joy.

And when they were come into the house, they saw the young child with Mary his mother, and fell down, and worshipped him: and when they had opened their treasures, they presented unto him gifts; gold, and frankincense, and myrrh.

Matthew 2: 1-11